THE
Hedgewitch's
LITTLE BOOK OF
Spells, Charms & Brews

© Sarah Coyne

ABOUT THE AUTHOR

Tudorbeth is the principal of the British College of Witch-craft and Wizardry and teaches courses on witchcraft. She is the author of numerous books, including *A Spellbook for the Seasons* (Eddison Books, 2019). Tudorbeth is a hereditary practitioner; her great grandmother was a well-known tea reader in Ireland while her Welsh great grandmother was a healer and wise woman.

THE
Hedgewitch's
LITTLE BOOK OF

Spells, Charms
& Brews

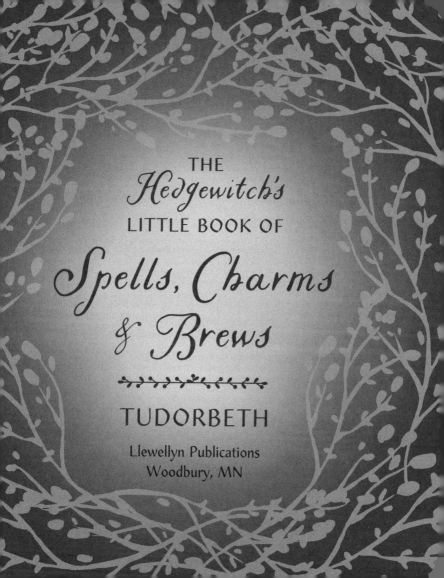

TUDORBETH

Llewellyn Publications
Woodbury, MN

FIRST EDITION
First Printing, 2021

Book design by Donna Burch-Brown
Cover design by Shira Atakpu
Interior art by the Llewellyn Art Department

Llewellyn Publications is a registered trademark of Llewellyn Worldwide Ltd.

Library of Congress Cataloging-in-Publication Data
Names: Tudorbeth, author.
Title: The hedgewitch's little book of spells, charms & brews / Tudorbeth.
Description: First edition. | Woodbury, Minnesota : Llewellyn Publications,
   [2021] | Includes bibliographical references.
Identifiers: LCCN 2020050501 (print) | LCCN 2020050502 (ebook) | ISBN
   9780738767451 (hardcover) | ISBN 9780738767512 (ebook)
Subjects: LCSH: Magic. | Charms. | Formulas, recipes, etc.
Classification: LCC BF1621 .T83 2021 (print) | LCC BF1621 (ebook) | DDC
   133.4/3—dc23
LC record available at https://lccn.loc.gov/2020050501
LC ebook record available at https://lccn.loc.gov/2020050502

Llewellyn Worldwide Ltd. does not participate in, endorse, or have any authority or responsibility concerning private business transactions between our authors and the public.

All mail addressed to the author is forwarded but the publisher cannot, unless specifically instructed by the author, give out an address or phone number.

Any internet references contained in this work are current at publication time, but the publisher cannot guarantee that a specific location will continue to be maintained. Please refer to the publisher's website for links to authors' websites and other sources.

Llewellyn Publications
A Division of Llewellyn Worldwide Ltd.
2143 Wooddale Drive
Woodbury, MN 55125-2989
www.llewellyn.com

Printed in China

DEDICATION

I dedicate this book to the Witch of Endor, Hypatia, Petronilla de Meath, Joan of Arc, Anne Boleyn, Helen Duncan, and all sisters and brothers whose lives have been destroyed by the hands of those who feared their strength, individuality, and power. Blessed be, sisters, and rest in peace.

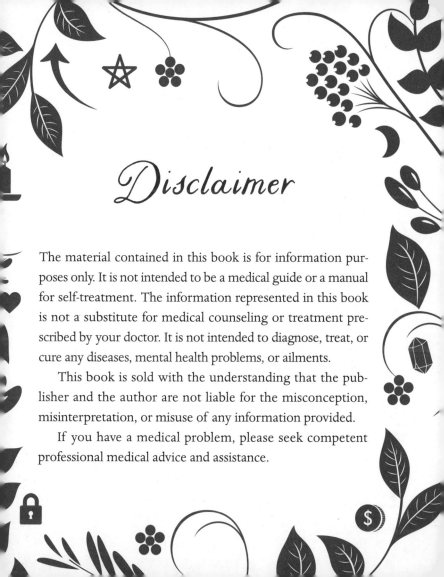

Disclaimer

The material contained in this book is for information purposes only. It is not intended to be a medical guide or a manual for self-treatment. The information represented in this book is not a substitute for medical counseling or treatment prescribed by your doctor. It is not intended to diagnose, treat, or cure any diseases, mental health problems, or ailments.

This book is sold with the understanding that the publisher and the author are not liable for the misconception, misinterpretation, or misuse of any information provided.

If you have a medical problem, please seek competent professional medical advice and assistance.

Contents

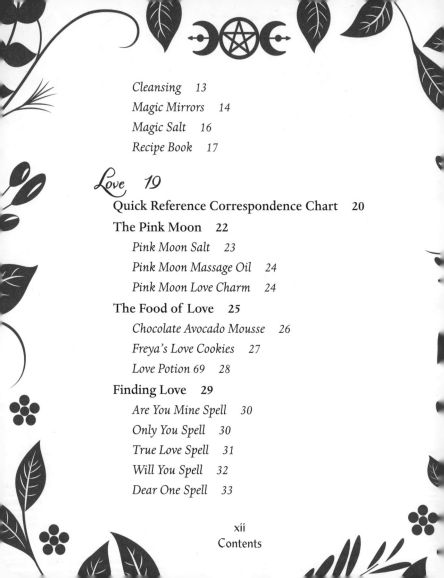

Contents

Contents

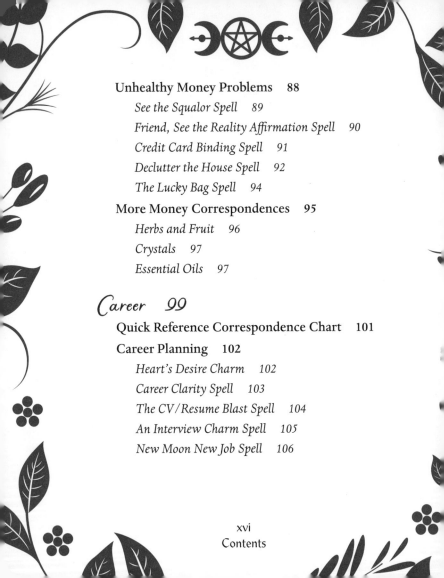

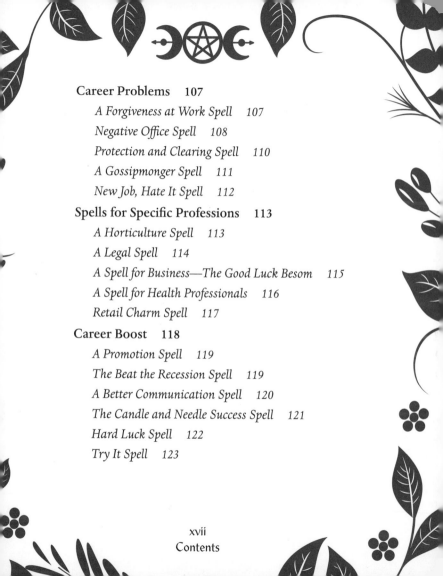

Contents

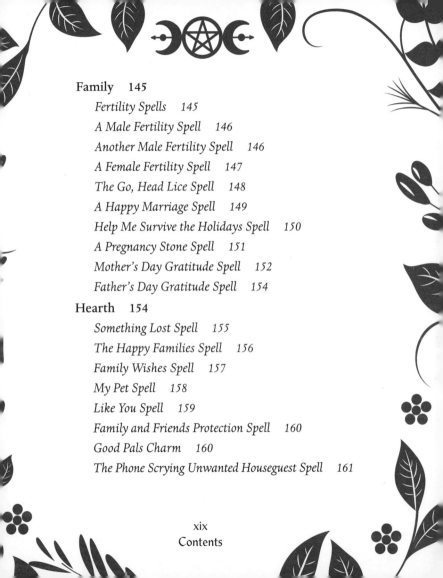

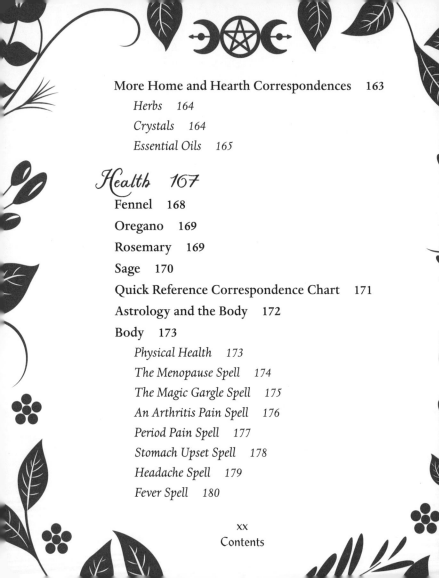

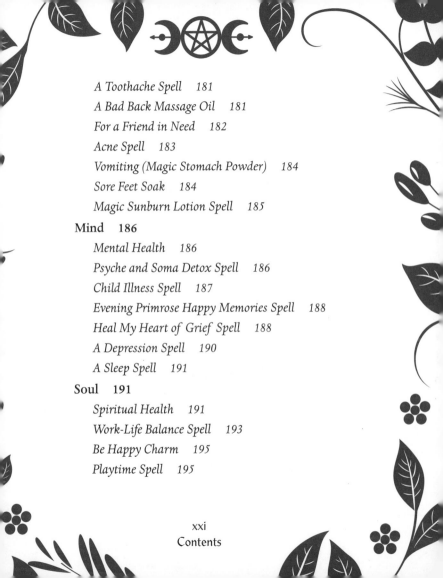

Contents

Seasonal Spells 223

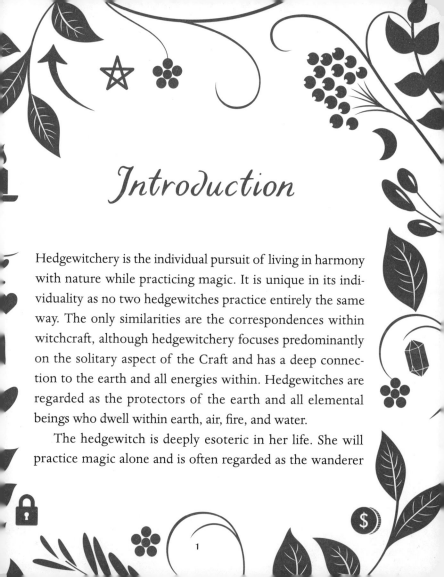

Introduction

Hedgewitchery is the individual pursuit of living in harmony with nature while practicing magic. It is unique in its individuality as no two hedgewitches practice entirely the same way. The only similarities are the correspondences within witchcraft, although hedgewitchery focuses predominantly on the solitary aspect of the Craft and has a deep connection to the earth and all energies within. Hedgewitches are regarded as the protectors of the earth and all elemental beings who dwell within earth, air, fire, and water.

The hedgewitch is deeply esoteric in her life. She will practice magic alone and is often regarded as the wanderer

between worlds. The term *hedgewitch* comes from the Saxon word *haegtessa*, which means "hedgerider." A hedge is that part of nature that divides one place from another and can consist of various plants, such as hawthorn, trees, shrubbery, roses, and all manner of flora.

However, the Saxon meaning of a hedge was somewhat different as it related to forests and not necessarily a garden fence made of plants. Forests were considered the unknown because they contained all spirits and creatures. They were dark and often dangerous places teeming with wolves, bears, bats, and many other animals that our ancient ancestors found frightening and foreboding.

In the time of the Saxon's ancestors, wise women and healers lived inside forests or just outside a forest. Therefore, the hedgewitch lived on the border of both worlds. She lived in a dangerous world of the unknown and knew every plant and tree of the forest, and yet she was also of the physical realm. She was both reality and the unknown world of magic, myth, and mystery.

My ancestors were of these women, and I have followed their solitary ways for many years. Traditionally, the path of the hedgewitch was considered a female path, but many families passed their knowledge down to their sons, who in turn passed it down to their own children. This knowledge consisted of herb lore and plant knowledge, whether for medicinal, culinary, or spiritual use and practice. It also consisted of the awareness of elemental spirits and the practices associated with them, such as leaving food out on a set night for the "wee folk" or tipping one's head at the first magpie of the day for good luck. Lessons were taught to respect nature and to never take her for granted. Magic was part of an accepted and vibrant reality integral to one's culture and mentality.

This little book of hedgewitchery intends to show how magic can be weaved into your life to allow the mystery of elemental nature craft into everyday living. I have kept many of the old spells but added new and more readily available ingredients. You will also learn one of the oldest spells in the world: the "candle and needle" spell, which can be used for any purpose you wish.

Spells are like prayers with the added kick of using nature to fuel them. Our intentions are cast out of us into

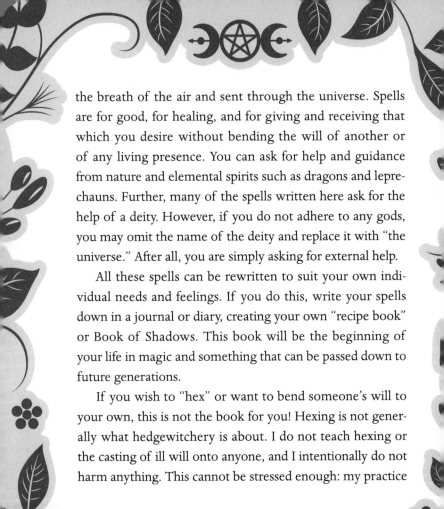

the breath of the air and sent through the universe. Spells are for good, for healing, and for giving and receiving that which you desire without bending the will of another or of any living presence. You can ask for help and guidance from nature and elemental spirits such as dragons and leprechauns. Further, many of the spells written here ask for the help of a deity. However, if you do not adhere to any gods, you may omit the name of the deity and replace it with "the universe." After all, you are simply asking for external help.

All these spells can be rewritten to suit your own individual needs and feelings. If you do this, write your spells down in a journal or diary, creating your own "recipe book" or Book of Shadows. This book will be the beginning of your life in magic and something that can be passed down to future generations.

If you wish to "hex" or want to bend someone's will to your own, this is not the book for you! Hexing is not generally what hedgewitchery is about. I do not teach hexing or the casting of ill will onto anyone, and I intentionally do not harm anything. This cannot be stressed enough: my practice

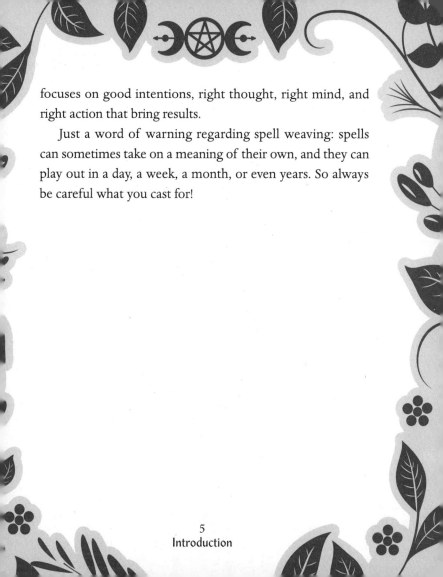

focuses on good intentions, right thought, right mind, and right action that bring results.

Just a word of warning regarding spell weaving: spells can sometimes take on a meaning of their own, and they can play out in a day, a week, a month, or even years. So always be careful what you cast for!

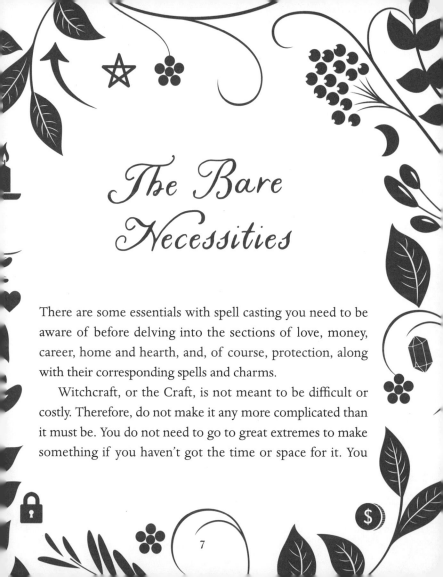

The Bare Necessities

There are some essentials with spell casting you need to be aware of before delving into the sections of love, money, career, home and hearth, and, of course, protection, along with their corresponding spells and charms.

Witchcraft, or the Craft, is not meant to be difficult or costly. Therefore, do not make it any more complicated than it must be. You do not need to go to great extremes to make something if you haven't got the time or space for it. You

do not have to pay large amounts of money for any articles or ingredients required for a spell. *You* yourself have all the power needed to achieve the outcome of your own spell. You can manifest all that you seek. I will merely show you one way, but the Craft may come to you in different ways. Always trust your own instincts and be your own guide.

BASIC PRACTICE ALTAR

Some spells call for you to perform them on or near your altar, but an altar can be anything from a special place to a special tree; it doesn't need to be a specific place in your home. It could be anywhere you feel is a sacred space where you won't be disturbed while performing a spell, such as out in the garden or on your balcony.

CORRESPONDENCES

Throughout this book, you will become familiar with this term. Correspondences form the central core of hedge-witchery and mean everything in this world and universe is connected. Correspondence was often explained to me as a giant spiderweb with strands shooting off here, there, and everywhere, but all strands are connected. These strands, or correspondences, are everything from colors to days to months to time itself.

Correspondences are also numbers, words, crystals, herbs, plants, trees, animals, insects, weather, clouds, planets, you, and me. Along with these correspondences are also the correspondences of the other realm: the elemental world of fairies, elves, pixies, Pegasus, salamanders, angels, sylphs, and all the other beings who are energies and manifestations of earth, air, fire, and water.

In each section of this book, there is a chart of correspondences for you to use when making your own spells.

Here is a chart of basic correspondences:

Monday: Moon, silver, moonstone, orris root, camphor, psychic

Tuesday: Mars, red, ruby, basil, cinnamon, physical

Wednesday: Mercury, yellow, opal, mandrake, bayberry, mental

Thursday: Jupiter, blue, amethyst, hyssop, sage, luck

Friday: Venus, green, emerald, hibiscus, rose, love

Saturday: Saturn, black, onyx, cypress, patchouli, karma

Sunday: Sun, gold, goldstone, frankincense, orange, success

DEITIES

I adhere to the gods and goddesses, and some feature in certain areas more prominently than others, especially in the money and health sections. Gods and goddesses are powerful beings to work with and for and are a great benefit.

MAGIC CUPBOARD

It's a good idea to store all the items you use for magic in a separate place as you develop within hedgewitchery. A shelf or even a box is a good place to store candles, oils, salt, crystals, and all other magical intentions. There are two reasons for this practice: it helps to develop respect for magic and all products used, and it keeps things "clean," as we do not want to cross-contaminate magical intentions, especially after we have spent time cleansing something before use.

SUPPLIES, TOOLS, AND OTHER HEDGEWITCH BASICS

Candles

Many spells call for us to anoint a candle, which means rubbing some of the stated essential oil onto the candle, including its sides and base. Using your index finger and thumb, dab the essential oil on the candle and rub up and down. Do not rub the oil onto the wick—just the sides and base.

The other thing to remember with candles is to never leave any candle unattended. Always make sure to extinguish it either with a candlesnuffer or by blowing it out as the spell requires. Many spells in my families' hedgewitchery require blowing out candles, as the power of the rising smoke carries wishes and spells to the other realm.

There is another tradition with candles, and that is to never throw out candles. The wax can be used again in another candle. The saying is, "Never throw out the light." Candles not only give us light, but they represent the divine light and sacred flame. Fire is a sacred element, as all the elements are.

Charms

A charm basically is a chant or incantation recited in order to produce some good or bad effect magically (the term *charm* means "to sing"). An object may be charmed in this manner, or the charm may be written down. Such charms when worn or carried are called "amulets."

Crystals

Crystals and semiprecious stones are a valuable resource that can be used for anything and everything. First, cleanse your crystal in some water with three pinches of magic salt (see page 16) and leave it for about an hour, then let it dry naturally. To charge or recharge your crystal, use the full moon or full sun. Leave the crystal in the light of either for a couple of hours, allowing the moon or sun's rays to charge your crystal.

Elixirs

An elixir is made by dropping a specific crystal in some water and allowing it to soak for a couple of hours. Remove the crystal before using the elixir.

Essential Oils

Always check with a medical practitioner before using oils if you are pregnant, have epilepsy, or have an allergy. Never use oils directly on your skin; for massage, always use at least ten drops of the base oil specified in the spell. Do not take essential oils internally unless stated. Also, be careful with sunlight after using oils as some are photosensitive.

Glass Bottles

Do not go to great expense buying fancy glass bottles for your oils, potions, or decoctions. Save your glass jars and mason jars! Wash them out and leave them until they are completely dry. Use glass paint to darken them, such as navy blue or deep red. You could color-code them: red for essential oils, and blue for oils to be used in cooking.

Cleansing

Lemon is a natural cleanser, and you can use it on almost anything, as you can with vinegar. We also use lemon and vinegar to consecrate and cleanse items and resources, from

crystals to utensils, because we do not want leftover residue from spells or other people—such as emotions and experiences—interfering in our own spells and magical intentions. Think of residue as spiritual viruses that can contaminate our good intentions.

There are several other ways to cleanse depending on the material of the item that needs cleansing. You can use incense for a book or paper-based product. Slowly waft the incense around the item. Let the item pass through the rising smoke. For crystals and anything that is not damaged by water, allow the item to soak for at least an hour in water.

Another way to cleanse is spritzing or spraying magical holy water. This water is made by mixing three teaspoons of magic salt and three drops of spikenard essential oil into a spray bottle containing clean water. Use as and when required.

Magic Mirrors
A mirror is a good resource to have, especially if you infuse it with a spell. Buy a small mirror in a frame, such as a mini

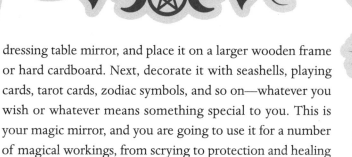

dressing table mirror, and place it on a larger wooden frame or hard cardboard. Next, decorate it with seashells, playing cards, tarot cards, zodiac symbols, and so on—whatever you wish or whatever means something special to you. This is your magic mirror, and you are going to use it for a number of magical workings, from scrying to protection and healing spells.

However, before you use the mirror, infuse it with your magic and say this spell over it:

> *Mirror, mirror, on the wall.*
> *Let me see the future of all.*
> *Give me sight, but do not fright.*
> *Mirror, mirror, enchant me.*
> *Mirror, mirror, so mote it be.*

When not in use, wrap your mirror in a dark cloth and store it in your magical cupboard. This is a resource that is only for magical use and is not to be used for everyday purposes.

Magic Salt

It is always a good idea to have a jar of magical salt in your magic cupboard, and it is very easy to make. Salt is sacred, extremely powerful, and embodies all the elements. It can come from the sea or from mines deep within the earth; it is therefore both of earth and of water. It is dried by the wind and is therefore also of the air. Put a couple of grains of salt on your tongue and taste it in its purity; it is sharp, and it burns, so it is also of fire. Salt can heal, and too much can kill. It is both a commodity and a necessity. Do not underestimate its power of good and its ability to do good.

Making magic salt is quite easy. On the night of a full moon, leave salt—either sea or mountain salt—out in the moonlight. Let the moon charge it with its energy. In the morning, place the salt in a clean jar and tie a white ribbon around it. This salt can now be used for absolutely everything from cooking to magical work.

Recipe Book

My family always called the book we wrote spells, remedies, and potions in "the recipe book." You may otherwise know it as the Book of Shadows or Grimoire. It is basically just an exercise book with a list of how-to guides and recipes. It is always wise to write down what spell you cast and its outcome as this information is good to look back on. It is also a helpful timeline to view how long a spell takes to come to fruition.

❖

All these supplies and tools are just examples for you to begin building up your hedgewitchery cupboard. You do not have to go to great expense to collect them; you will probably already have quite a few of them around your home.

Now that you have the basics, you can begin casting some basic spells. Remember most of all to cast with love in your heart and embrace the magic.

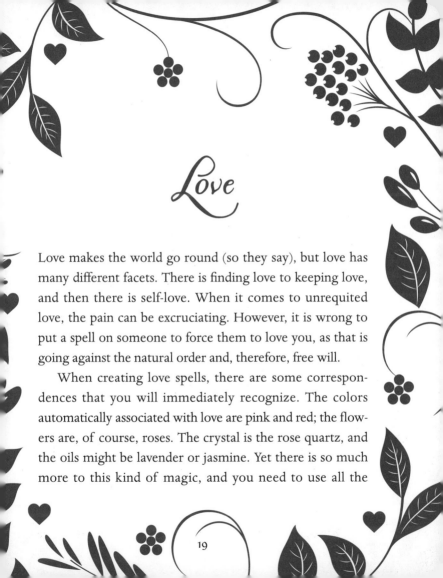

Love

Love makes the world go round (so they say), but love has many different facets. There is finding love to keeping love, and then there is self-love. When it comes to unrequited love, the pain can be excruciating. However, it is wrong to put a spell on someone to force them to love you, as that is going against the natural order and, therefore, free will.

When creating love spells, there are some correspondences that you will immediately recognize. The colors automatically associated with love are pink and red; the flowers are, of course, roses. The crystal is the rose quartz, and the oils might be lavender or jasmine. Yet there is so much more to this kind of magic, and you need to use all the

QUICK REFERENCE
CORRESPONDENCE CHART

Colors	red and pink
Crystals	rose quartz
Flower	rose
Incense	rose or jasmine
Oil	rose or jasmine
Day	Friday
Deities	Venus or Aphrodite
Planet	Venus
Numbers	6 or 9

appropriate correspondences to create the right vibrations for the desired effects and outcomes.

While there are some correspondences for love that are generic, others are more specific. For example, red candles represent health, energy, strength, courage, and sexual potency, and pink candles are for love, affection, and romance. Similarly, some spells and charms are specific, but others are generic, which means they can be used for all those who are seeking love or wish to enhance the love they have.

The planetary and time correspondences for love are the moon and the planet Venus, which was named after the ancient Roman goddess. Her ruling day is Friday; therefore, love spells are best performed on that day in order to align the magical workings with further power.

There are also number correspondences for love, and the main two are six and nine. Six is the number of love (and responsibility), whereas nine is the number of romance (and artistic genius). A lot of the spells described in this chapter will feature six ingredients or use six quantities.

In addition to the correspondences listed here, there is another section at the end of this chapter for correspondences

that can be used as substitutions in each of the spells or to create your own spell entirely.

THE PINK MOON

In witchcraft, the moon has typically been represented as female, nurturing, and something that governs emotions. In the area of love, pink moon salt is a perfect accompaniment to many spells.

The pink full moon occurs around the month of April and is called that because of wild ground phlox, which is one of the first flowers of spring to appear. However, there are other times of the year when a pink moon, or super moon, occurs—usually around the times of the equinoxes in either September or March. It also happens during an eclipse, which creates an amazing effect.

The moon is powerful enough in its own right, but when extra celestial events happen, these trigger greater power and potency for our spells and magic.

Pink Moon Salt

Pink moon salt is perfect for all spells regarding love and sex. The pink moon's heightened power gives an extra boost to the salt and increases its potency. If you can, use Himalayan pink salt; its color gives it an extra boost in love.

On the night of the full moon, place the salt into a bowl and leave it on a window ledge. Hold your hands up in the air and say these words:

Blessed moon on this night.
Bless this salt with your light.

Leave the salt in view of the moon's rays all night. In the morning, put the salt in an airtight container, like a clean jam jar. Place a pink ribbon around it.

You can now use this salt for all magical purposes, from magical bath salts to cooking. Use the salt in your meals for an aphrodisiac kick in your food.

Pink Moon Massage Oil

There is nothing more sensual than a body massage, especially when it is enhanced by the power of the pink moon.

Use a carrier oil, such as almond oil, and put three drops each of cinnamon essential oil, rose essential oil, and lotus essential oil in a little dark glass bottle with the carrier oil. Use as much carrier oil as you wish depending on how much you need. Shake the bottle to mix the oils together and say these words:

> *Three times three,*
> *pink moon, I call to thee.*
> *Grant my pleasure to my love and me.*
> *An' it harm none, so mote it be.*

Pink Moon Love Charm

Create love in your house all year round by crafting a love charm infused with the power of the pink moon. You will need the following:

2 cinnamon sticks

1 teaspoon of anise oil

1 teaspoon of honey

2 drops of musk oil

Rose petals

A pinch of catnip

On the night of the pink full moon, mix the oils, honey, and catnip together, and then soak the cinnamon sticks in the mixture with the rose petals for a couple of hours before leaving the sticks to dry. Tie the cinnamon sticks together with a pink ribbon and hang them up in a place where you desire love to be. You can also tie rose petals in with the cinnamon sticks if you wish.

THE FOOD OF LOVE

There are many ways to create the mood for love, and one of the oldest is an aphrodisiac. General food aphrodisiacs accredited with the power of sexual excitement are celery, asparagus, and mushrooms; ginger, garlic, peppers, vanilla, cloves, borage, and rue are herbs and spices that can also be effective. Additionally, lavender, oysters, chocolate, and rosemary are basic aphrodisiac compounds.

Chocolate Avocado Mousse

1 avocado

1 hot chocolate mix (or about 3–4 tablespoons of pure cocoa powder)

Peel and quarter a ripe avocado, removing the stone, and chop it up into cubes. Place the ingredients together in a blender or hand mixer and blend them until the mousse is smooth and no dry cocoa powder remains. As it blends, say,

> *Bring now my love to me.*
> *Complete in sweet love's harmony.*
> *Bring romance tonight.*
> *Magic mousse, make our love right.*

Then leave the mousse in the fridge and serve when the time is right. This can be made a day in advance, but do not leave it for more than a day. There are many other ingredients you could add to the mousse: chocolate chips, cinnamon, ginger, bananas, a teaspoon of instant coffee (for a mocha taste), coconut, nuts, a tablespoon of lavender liquor—the possibilities are endless. You could melt a bar of chocolate and pour it over the dish for pure decadence. It all depends on your budget, taste, and imagination.

Freya's Love Cookies

   100 grams (4 ounces) of flour

   100 grams (4 ounces) of butter

   50 grams (2 ounces) of sugar

   1 egg yolk

   The rind of half a lemon

   ½ teaspoon of baking powder

   ½ teaspoon of saffron

   50 grams (2 ounces) of chopped cherries

Cream the butter and sugar together. Add the lemon rind and chopped cherries and beat in the yolk. Add flour, baking powder, and saffron, and mix. Roll out the dough and cut it with a heart-shaped cutter. Bake it in a hot oven (425°F/220°C) for fifteen to twenty minutes. Take it out, then leave it to cool. Enjoy. You could indulge further by dipping half the heart biscuit in melted chocolate and leaving it to set before enjoying.

As you stir the mixture deasil, or clockwise, say these words:

Bring together my love and me.
Together in love's sweet harmony.

Saffron and cherries are perfect companions for love spells—equal amounts of passion and love are an excellent combination.

Love Potion 69

1 bottle of sweet red wine (or a 1-liter carton of any red juice, such as cherry or red grape)

1 ginseng root cut into 6 equal pieces

6 drops of vanilla extract

6 drops of strawberry juice

6 drops of apple juice

6 basil leaves

6 red rose petals

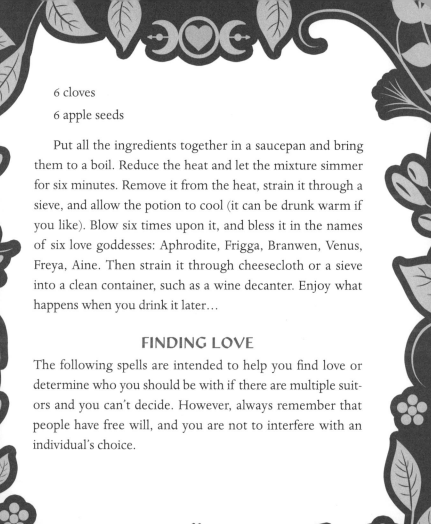

6 cloves

6 apple seeds

Put all the ingredients together in a saucepan and bring them to a boil. Reduce the heat and let the mixture simmer for six minutes. Remove it from the heat, strain it through a sieve, and allow the potion to cool (it can be drunk warm if you like). Blow six times upon it, and bless it in the names of six love goddesses: Aphrodite, Frigga, Branwen, Venus, Freya, Aine. Then strain it through cheesecloth or a sieve into a clean container, such as a wine decanter. Enjoy what happens when you drink it later…

FINDING LOVE

The following spells are intended to help you find love or determine who you should be with if there are multiple suitors and you can't decide. However, always remember that people have free will, and you are not to interfere with an individual's choice.

Are You Mine Spell

This spell requires a white rose and for you to sleep and dream of your intended.

Before you go to bed, hold a white rose in your hand carefully, as not to be pricked. Say this spell:

> Flower of elegance, rose of white.
> Power of love I seek this night.
> White for clarity, white so clear.
> Make me dream of him/her/them I hold dear.

Place the rose under your pillow and allow yourself to dream of your intended. In your dream, ask your beloved if they are yours. If you do not dream of them at all, then there is your answer as well.

Only You Spell

Create this spell by placing an incantation on someone's photo. Remember, it is wrong to force a person to do something they do not want to do. That said, this spell will last for a brief time so that the person thinks of you, and perhaps things will happen naturally from there.

Print a recent photograph of your intended and a photograph of you. Roll the two photos together and bind them with red thread. As you begin winding the thread around the photos, think of your beloved and say,

> It is not the thread that I'm winding,
> it is love, only yours for me and mine for you.

Do not cut the thread. Keep the photos and thread together in your underwear drawer for seven nights. After seven nights, dispose of the photos and thread by burying them in the garden or window box—somewhere the earth can dispose of them gradually. Give thanks as you bury them.

True Love Spell

Light a pink candle on a Friday night at 6:00 p.m. (remember, Friday is the day of Venus, who is the goddess of love, and

we want her to help us as much as possible with this). Say these words into the flame:

> *Send my love to me.*
> *Smoke from this candle, rise.*
> *Bring him/her/them to me.*
> *A gift from heaven's eyes.*

Imagine your true love and you together, then blow out the candle and watch the smoke rise upward to the universe.

Will You Spell

We never interfere with free will. We can only ask the question. Help someone with making a decision with this spell.

Have a picture of the person you wish to ask in front of you, and light a white candle. Sprinkle salt in a circle around the photo and say,

> *Wisdom followed through actions and thoughts.*
> *Make the decision that I seek.*
> *Be strong, not meek.*

If you go, I set you free.
An' it harm none, so mote it be.

Dear One Spell

If there is someone you have been thinking of, then cast this spell. Lift up your arms to make a *Y* shape and say,

Heaven above, bring me my love.
The dear one who holds my heart.
Forever together, let us never part.
Round and round we go.
Where our love stops, nobody knows.

Don't Know Who Spell

If you are between multiple partners and can't decide whom to be with, cast this very old spell using just an apple.

Peel the apple, keeping the peel in one piece. Blow on it and give it a kiss. Turn around widdershins (anticlockwise) three times and throw the peel over your left shoulder. The letter suggested by the shape of the peel when it lands on the ground is the initial of your true love.

New Love Spell

If you have been without love for quite some time, try this spell. For six mornings, when you first begin to open your eyes, fill your head with thoughts of love. Then say this spell nine times:

> *May I find the love I seek.*
> *May the love I seek find me.*
> *An' it harm none, so mote it be.*

All Mine Spell

Take a pin and write your intended's name into one red candle, one pink candle, and one white candle. Set the three candles into a triangle. Say these words:

> *I love you.*
> *You love me.*
> *Happy together.*
> *We both shall be.*

Light the candles, focus on the light they make, and imagine your beloved's face appearing in the center of the three candles. Say the spell again. Say the spell four more times before you place your intent upon your breath, then blow out the candles.

The Ideal Love Spell

Find a picture of your ideal person to love in a magazine and cut it out. Crunch some lavender over the picture as you say these words:

> *I conjure thee.*
> *Sweet love and harmony.*
> *Just as you are, right in front of me.*
> *I conjure thee.*
> *Come to me.*
> *An' it harm none, so mote it be.*

Roll up the picture with the lavender and place it in an envelope. Keep it in a secret place.

Lovebug Charm

Create a lovebug charm to carry in your purse or wallet all the time to have someone fall in love with you.

Cut a circle the size of a small bottle lid from scarlet cardstock. Draw four dots on it. With each dot, think of an attribute your ideal lover will have (beauty, wealth, a sense of humor, a protective nature, charm, sensitivity, etc.).

Name each spot with the attributes you select.

After, hold the lovebug in both hands, close your eyes, and say,

> *Aphrodite, hear my plea.*
> *Let my ideal love come to me.*
> *Little lovebug, bring my true love to me.*

Keep the lovebug charm in your purse or wallet and see what happens.

KEEPING LOVE ALIVE SPELLS

Love can be tricky to keep alive due to our daily lives, which can be so hectic. It is easy to fall out of love with someone when work dictates what little time you have. Use these spells to fall in love all over again with that special someone, and keep love alive by doing those little things you know they like.

The King and Queen Spell

Here is an old and exquisite spell. You will need the king and queen chess pieces. They can be either black or white. Although this is called the "king and queen" spell, this is a sign of respect to the past. In the actual practice of the spell, you could have two king pieces or two queen pieces to represent the couple and whatever gender is in the relationship. As an alternative to chess pieces, you could use playing cards, such as the queen of hearts, and so on.

This is a good spell if you are having trouble in the relationship and no one is communicating very well. Place one royal at one end of a shelf, a mantelpiece, or even a room, and place the other royal opposite to the first. Say these words:

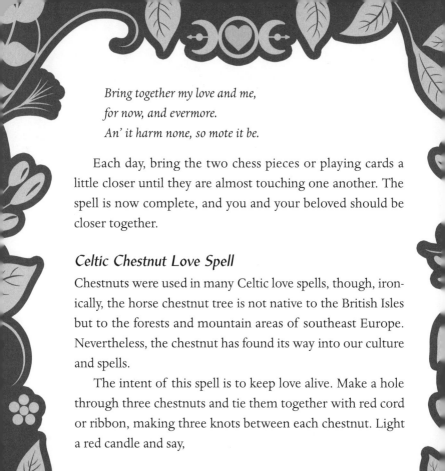

Bring together my love and me,
for now, and evermore.
An' it harm none, so mote it be.

Each day, bring the two chess pieces or playing cards a little closer until they are almost touching one another. The spell is now complete, and you and your beloved should be closer together.

Celtic Chestnut Love Spell

Chestnuts were used in many Celtic love spells, though, ironically, the horse chestnut tree is not native to the British Isles but to the forests and mountain areas of southeast Europe. Nevertheless, the chestnut has found its way into our culture and spells.

The intent of this spell is to keep love alive. Make a hole through three chestnuts and tie them together with red cord or ribbon, making three knots between each chestnut. Light a red candle and say,

Lord and lady of light and dark,
grant love forevermore to my partner and me.
To couples everywhere, blessed be.
An' it harm none, so mote it be.

Keep the chestnut charm in a safe place for a year, then bury it in a garden, giving thanks to the lord and lady.

Don't Cry Charm

This is often called "the hankie charm" as it involves precisely that: a hankie.

Place four drops of eucalyptus essential oil onto a cotton hankie and say,

Do not weep and do not cry.
Through tears, try to see.
You are everything to me.

Give the hankie to someone you care for—a love, family member, or friend—when they are upset.

Cuddle Me Spell

Use this spell if you need a cuddle and the one you love is not catching your vibes. Say these words under your breath:

> *Cuddle me snuggly,*
> *cuddle me quick.*
> *I need you now.*
> *So, quick, quick, quick.*

Yes Dear Spell

Always be there for someone you hold dear, no matter how far away you are. Light a purple candle and say into the flame,

> *Yes, my dear.*
> *I will be near.*
> *When you need me the most, I will be.*
> *An' it harm none, so mote it be.*

Write a letter to them or send a little gift through the post to let them know you are thinking of them and will

always be there for them, even if you haven't spoken in a while or have had a fight.

SEX SPELLS

Similar to the above love spells, the physical act of love can be enhanced by spell weaving.

Light the Passion Spell

Say this spell three times a night for five nights in a row. Light a red candle and lover's incense of jasmine, amber, or lotus oil. Then say,

> *I am possessed by the burning love for [name].*
> *This love comes to me from Aphrodite.*
> *Let [name] desire me if it be.*
> *I am his/hers/theirs and he/she/they is/are mine.*
> *Let our bodies be entwined.*
> *With this connection divine.*
> *An' it harm none, so mote it be.*

Lust Scorching Spell

If you really need to ignite the passion and just want to get completely lost in pure lust, then cast this spell. Light six red candles and say this spell three times:

> *Goddess Venus, send your sensual might.*
> *May your passion burn bright.*
> *Lust-filled sex I yearn tonight.*
> *Goddess Venus, grant this to me.*
> *An' it harm none, so mote it be.*

Leave the candles burning while making love, but be sure to blow them out before you go to sleep.

Condom Spell

After lighting two purple candles and musk incense, hold the condoms in your hand and focus on your goal. Visualize yourself meeting interesting, sexy people and having your pick of the bunch. Then open your eyes and focus on the flames. Say,

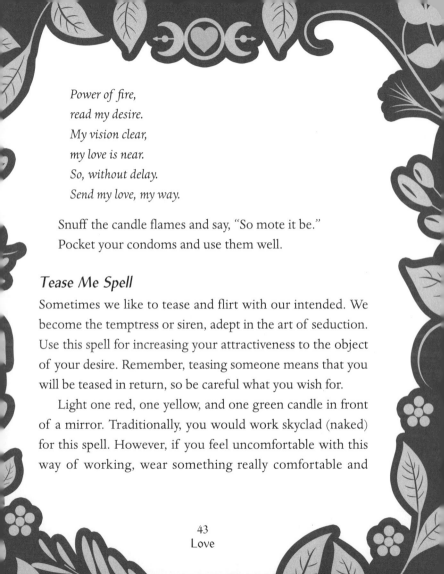

Power of fire,
read my desire.
My vision clear,
my love is near.
So, without delay.
Send my love, my way.

Snuff the candle flames and say, "So mote it be."
Pocket your condoms and use them well.

Tease Me Spell

Sometimes we like to tease and flirt with our intended. We become the temptress or siren, adept in the art of seduction. Use this spell for increasing your attractiveness to the object of your desire. Remember, teasing someone means that you will be teased in return, so be careful what you wish for.

Light one red, one yellow, and one green candle in front of a mirror. Traditionally, you would work skyclad (naked) for this spell. However, if you feel uncomfortable with this way of working, wear something really comfortable and loose, such as your favorite lounging suit or joggers. Then, kneeling in front of the mirror and candles, say these words to your reflection:

> For near and far, I attract him/her/them.
> He/she/they will hear my call.
> Overcome with willful desire.
> Only I can quench his/her/their fire.
> I am passion, I am love.
> My sex is sent from above.
> Hear me, feel me, tease me, please.
> An' it harm none, so mote it be.

BEAUTY AND LOVE

Makeup is big business. We can use lipsticks and eyeshadows to enhance our looks and captivate someone, just as the makeup companies intended, but we can also use magic as an added allure to capture the heart of someone.

Red Lipstick

Today, we think that wearing red lipstick is sexy. In ancient times, it was viewed as a form of protection. Red lipstick is believed to ward off evil spirits and negative energies.

Sweet Kiss Spell

Buy some strawberry, cherry, or any sweet fruit-flavored lip balm and hold it in your hands as if in prayer. Close your eyes and say,

> *Sweet kisses divine.*
> *Whose lips only kiss mine.*
> *Sweet tender lips so pure.*
> *Let us kiss forevermore.*

Every time you wear your lip balm, your partner will think only of you.

True Love Lips Spell

Use this spell for only your lover's lips. Every time you wear your lipstick, your lover will want to kiss your lips.

Find the brightest scarlet lipstick and apply it to your lips. Then, on a white piece of paper, pucker up and kiss the paper, leaving your lips' kissing shape. Then say,

> *My lips are divine, sweet as wine.*
> *Kiss no others', only mine.*

Then hide the kiss in his/her/their underwear drawer.

Eyeshadow Spell

If you would like a new admirer, try this spell. Sit in front of your mirror, and as you apply your eyeshadow, say,

> *Green shadow, blue shadow.*
> *Gold and silver, too.*
> *Send me a love that's new.*

TROUBLE IN LOVE

In today's world, there are many forces couples face, from stresses at work, to finances, family, and children. Relationships are hard to begin with, but with the ever-mounting pressures of a world that demands more and more of our time, our love lives can become our last thought. Things can turn wrong, and a toxic relationship can begin.

If you are unsure if you are in a toxic relationship, answer these questions:

- Do you want to spend time with that person?
- Do you feel happy and energized when you have been with them?
- Do you feel drained and exhausted after being with them?
- Do you agree with their comments and/or behavior?
- Do they make you cringe?

You can't choose your family,
but you can choose your friends and lovers.

What follows is a series of spells that help you come to terms with negative relationships. The first spell is to help a friend recognize the toxic qualities of their relationship.

Friend in Trouble Spell

You will need a photograph of your friend and a bowl of water. The reason why we use water in many love spells is because water is the element of emotions and time. Water is fluid, just like love, and can flow anywhere and be everywhere; there are no limitations or exceptions.

Place the photograph under the bowl of water and visualize your friend in happier times. Over the bowl of water, say,

> *Water lies before me.*
> *Help my friend see clarity.*
> *An' it harm none, so mote it be.*

Allow a couple of days for the spell to take effect. Your friend may start questioning themselves over the relationship or start to complain about little things their lover or partner is doing. This means the spell is taking effect. If they do not start commenting on the nature of their relationship, then simply perform the spell again.

See the Light Spell

If you are experiencing negativity in your relationship and yet feel bound and unable to see the whole picture, perform this spell when you are alone.

Light a white candle and meditate upon the flame. Watch how far the light radiates out from the candle, illuminating the darkness that surrounds it. When you feel ready, calm, and collected, repeat these words three times:

> *I am blind and cannot see.*
> *The binds holding me.*
> *Let me see the light.*
> *So that I can do what's right.*

After, think about your relationship. You could write in your journal about the negative ways your lover or partner makes you feel and about the things they do to upset you. Then begin to make plans to rectify the situation and set them in motion.

The Argument Spell

This spell is all about making up after an argument. It is inevitable that there will be arguments in any relationship. Candles have a calming effect, so you're going to light a specific candle to clear the air. Make a lavender-colored candle with four drops of lavender oil in it. As you make the candle, say over it,

> Candle fire, candle bright,
> ease our arguments this night.
> Differences make constant fights.
> Help us to see,
> the love between my partner and me.
> An' it harm none, so mote it be.

When you and your partner are together, light the candle and talk things through.

Healthy in Love Spell

Although it is wonderful to be in love, sometimes people begin to lose who they are individually while in a relationship. Remember that, even when together, you both are also individual souls. Recognize each other's individuality by performing this spell together.

Light a blue candle and have a photograph of the two of you together. Then both of you say into the photograph,

> *We two are one.*
> *But you are you and I am me.*
> *United we are but do not lose our individuality.*

Afterward, blow out the candle and watch the smoke rise upward toward the universe. Talk to each other about your differences and acknowledge them with respect.

Just Say No Spell

If you are trying to give something up as it is a bad habit (and that can also include people!), cast this spell on a waning moon.

> *Go away from me.*
> *I have no need.*
> *You are bad, so let me be.*

Whenever you are confronted with temptation, recite this spell over and over again.

Bye-Bye Spell

To say goodbye to a toxic friend or lover, use this spell. Write on a piece of paper the name of the person you want to say goodbye to.

Light a purple candle, roll up the paper in your left hand, and say into the flame,

> *[Name], I let you go with peace and love.*
> *Release the bonds from above.*
> *You go your way, and I go mine.*
> *Nevermore to meet in any time.*

Blow out the candle and watch the smoke rise. This is your toxic friend or lover leaving, detaching from you. Let them go.

I Surrender Spell

Sometimes we must surrender ourselves to whatever is causing the battle.

In front of your magic mirror, say these words:

Surrender, surrender, surrender I.
No more the battle cry.
Accept me as I am.
Though know I am no lamb.

Stare into the mirror and see your reflection. Look behind your reflection's shoulder and watch to see if an image forms behind you, indicating the change in you.

Declutter My Heart Spell

Sort out all the gifts an ex-lover has given you. Place the items in front of you or lay them out on the kitchen table. Light some patchouli incense and waft the incense over and around the items while repeating three times,

No more you and I.
As our love does die.
These objects are nothing to me.
Go now and be free.

One man's rubbish is another man's treasure.
Go now and give others pleasure.

Imagine the items in front of you going somewhere else and being enjoyed by other people. This way, you are not cursing the objects with your negativity from the relationship that ended badly.

After you have performed this spell, disperse the items in the usual way. Sell them or give them away to friends, a charity, or a thrift store. And be happy to do so.

SELF-LOVE

We are often taught to think of others before ourselves and that any form of self-love is selfish. However, if we don't look after ourselves, how can we possibly look after others? If we don't love ourselves first, how can we possibly love others? Self-love is all about looking after ourselves, listening to our own needs, and showing love to ourselves. When we love ourselves, we can start taking care of others and loving others as we would want to be loved.

Just Me Spell

After a difficult and hectic time, you just need some "me" time. Create a spa of sanctuary and calm in your bathroom. Using Epsom salts will ease the toxins out of your body and help heal your heart.

Run a warm salt bath, then soak in it. Say this spell:

> *All alone I am,*
> *here on my own.*
> *Space and free,*
> *peace return to me.*

Embrace the freedom in a space that is all your own. Imagine floating in an ocean of the purest blue, healing your mind and body.

Mermaid Me Spell

The legacy of the water elemental we know as "the mermaid" is taking care of oneself. She is all about feeling good about herself. If you want to connect with the spirit of the mermaids in general, turn your bathroom into a spa, a watery domain of indulgence. The colors of the merpeople are, of course, blues, whites, and greens—the colors of the oceans. You could also try to make your own shower and bath products and your own soaps. You do not have to go to great expense, as there are many kits available on the internet that include the soap, essential oils, colors, and molds at very reasonable prices.

Create your own "mermaid basket" of handmade beauty products—such as shell-shaped soaps, shower gels, bath salts, body scrubs, and shampoos—complete with a mermaid candle. This basket is just for you to use when you need that little extra love.

The stones and crystals we use to connect with the merpeople are larimar, or the stone of Atlantis, water sapphire, paua shell, and, of course, pearls. Another lesser-known stone for connection to merpeople is neptunite, which is named after the Roman god of the sea, Neptune (though this stone is rather rare and very expensive).

The essential oils to use in candles and bath or shower products are sandalwood, eucalyptus, cherry blossom, vanilla, hyacinth, and lilac. Just add a few drops of any of these essential oils in your chosen products.

Above all, learn to love yourself, which is easier said than done. Yet think of the wonderful merpeople and how free they are. Live for yourself, at least for a little while, and be free.

If you want to connect with the mermaid and self-love, run a warm bath and use the mermaid products you have bought or made. You will also need your magic mirror. As you soak in the bath, say these words:

> I call upon the watery deep,
> mermaids wonder and leap.
> Show me how to love me.
> Teach me thy tricks of beauty.

Lie still in the bath and close your eyes. Imagine mermaids leaping out of the water and talking to you. Watch them brushing their hair and looking into their mirrors, admiring themselves. Open your eyes and look into your mirror. Don't just look at the reflection, but all over, especially behind your shoulder. If you see sparks or glimmers of different light, know the elementals have heard you.

＊

This concludes the love section. What should be apparent from the spells here is that love in our world is neither black nor white—nor pink and red, for that matter. In literal terms, these spells can use a veritable rainbow of colors, from the pink moon salt, which has a pink-orange hue, to the white and yellow roses in the Are You Mine spell; from the lavenders and purples of the Bye-Bye spell to the blues and sea greens when working with the elementals of the sea, mermaids. When it comes to love in our world, it is a rainbow of possibility, but one that is born out of the right intent and respect for not only each other, but for ourselves.

ADDITIONAL LOVE SPELL INGREDIENTS

Here are some additional correspondences you can use in your spells. These items can be substituted for those listed in the spells in this love section as their harmonics work well together.

Herbs and Fruit

Apples are used in spells for love and healing. The core of the fruit is a natural pentagram.

Cardamom can be used for spells of love and lust.

Cumin is an herb that has been used for centuries by women as an aid for conception.

Fenugreek is an herb with the delightful nickname "breast enhancer." It was often given to women in harems. You can still get it in herbal food shops in pill or tea form.

Lavender is one of the most popular ingredients in love spells. The fragrant plant is also used by midwives to ease childbirth.

Liverwort is used in spells for love and protection.

Mandrake is believed to be the most magical herb of all. The mandrake root is the most powerful herb in love magic—as well as one of the deadliest, so take care.

Rosemary is an herb of love enchantment and can be used in spells provoking lust.

Crystals

Clear quartz is the master healing crystal, but it also brings balance, harmony, and love. This is a crystal that can be used particularly for male love spells.

Magnetite is a dark, granular-looking stone formed from iron, and, because it is magnetic, it is regarded as the ideal stone for attracting love and developing a balanced relationship. Male-to-male spells and charms are also improved when using this stone.

Rose quartz is the stone of unconditional love. It also opens the heart chakra.

Rhodochrosite is a stone that attracts love.

Soul mate crystal is two clear crystals of similar size growing from a common base. Place it in the farthest right-hand corner from the door in your bedroom.

Essential Oils

Aniseed oil was used by the ancients for massage. It is good for male spells.

Cinnamon oil has been used as an aphrodisiac. The oil was sprinkled over beds for a good, energetic night.

Lotus oil is used as an aphrodisiac. If you can get your hands on some, it's definitely worth it!

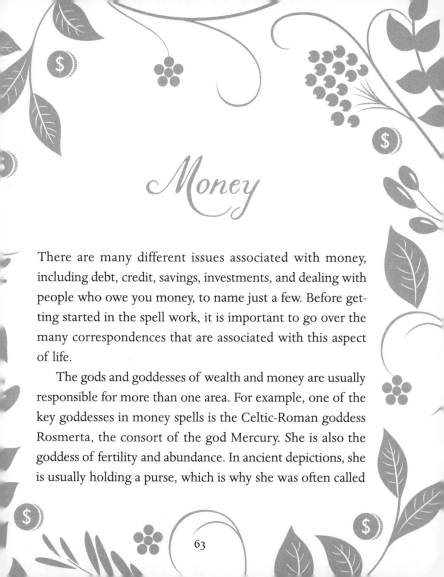

Money

There are many different issues associated with money, including debt, credit, savings, investments, and dealing with people who owe you money, to name just a few. Before getting started in the spell work, it is important to go over the many correspondences that are associated with this aspect of life.

The gods and goddesses of wealth and money are usually responsible for more than one area. For example, one of the key goddesses in money spells is the Celtic-Roman goddess Rosmerta, the consort of the god Mercury. She is also the goddess of fertility and abundance. In ancient depictions, she is usually holding a purse, which is why she was often called upon to help with money issues. Mercury himself is the Roman god of financial gain, commerce, communication, and luck, among other things, so he is a very valuable god to be aware of when dealing with money matters. The other gods and goddesses for money and wealth are Juno, Abundantia, Hermes, and Plutus (not to be confused with Pluto, also a god of wealth). We also have Cernunnos, who was a Celtic god of wealth. In Norse religion, the viking Njord was a very wealthy god who granted land and wealth to worthy people, so he's one worth remembering, too.

The correspondences in this money section are varied. The colors used in wealth spells are typically green, silver, gold, and yellow. The oils and herbs to use are saffron, mint, ginger, basil, nutmeg, lemon balm, honeysuckle, cinnamon, marjoram, and bay.

A word of warning with money magic: never tell anyone you are casting a spell for money. It's a bit like making a wish on a birthday cake candle—you are never meant to tell anyone, as then the wish won't come true. Money magic is a bit like that.

QUICK REFERENCE
CORRESPONDENCE CHART

Colors	green and gold
Crystals	citrine and goldstone
Flower	honeysuckle
Incense	cinnamon
Oil	mint
Day	Friday
Deities	Venus or Aphrodite
Planet	Venus
Numbers	5 or 6

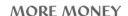

MORE MONEY

Most of us could use a bit of extra money at the end of the month—or at the beginning, for that matter. This set of spells is intended especially for that. Always ask for exactly what you need, and don't be greedy. If you are greedy and request more than you need, things might turn worse, so be careful what and how much you ask for.

A Money Pot Potion

Here is a lovely little money potion. However, it only lasts for fourteen days, so make sure you date the jar.

> 1 teaspoon of cinnamon
> 1 teaspoon of bay leaves
> 1 teaspoon of basil
> 1 teaspoon of marjoram

Grind the ingredients together with a pestle and mortar, and while doing so, say these words:

> *Money, money, money,*
> *come to me.*
> *An' it harm none, so mote it be.*

Stir four times and put the potion in a jar with a tight lid (such as a clean coffee jar). Keep the jar near your finances—for example, your bank book or credit cards. Remember to keep the potion for only fourteen days.

The Square of Venus

The Square of Venus is very good for money spells. If you add up all the numbers horizontally, vertically, or diagonally, they equal 175. Breaking this number down to $1 + 7 + 5$, we get 13, and $1 + 3$ is 4, the number of money and wealth. It is called the Square of Venus in honor of the goddess Venus as she is not only the goddess of love, but also of finance and money.

Write out the Square of Venus on green cardstock or paper. Do this spell on a Friday night as Venus governs that day. We are going to ask the goddess Venus for some financial help. Write the amount of money you would like on a piece of paper and put it on top of the Square of Venus. Say these words as you do so:

Goddess Venus, help me please.
This amount of money I need.

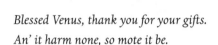

Blessed Venus, thank you for your gifts.
An' it harm none, so mote it be.

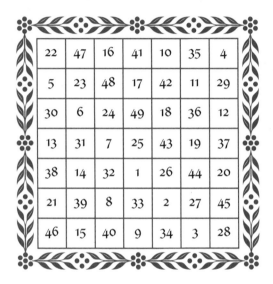

22	47	16	41	10	35	4
5	23	48	17	42	11	29
30	6	24	49	18	36	12
13	31	7	25	43	19	37
38	14	32	1	26	44	20
21	39	8	33	2	27	45
46	15	40	9	34	3	28

Leave the paper on the Square of Venus all night. In the morning, fold the paper four times and place it in a drawer. If nothing happens in about a week, do this ritual again for seven nights.

A Money Candle Spell

Anoint a green candle with one drop each of mint, basil, bay, and cinnamon. Put a needle halfway into the candle (you can choose where on the candle you want to stick the needle), and as you do so, imagine the amount of money you want to come to you. Light the candle and say these words:

> Money, money, come to me.
> Burning flame, let it be.
> An' it harm none, so mote it be.

The spell takes effect when the flame reaches the needle.

The Check It Out Spell

If you have a checkbook, fill out a blank check with the amount of money you desire. Put one drop each of basil, mint, saffron, and marjoram essential oils on the check and fold it in four. While folding, say these words:

> North, south, east, west,
> four quarters, I implore.
> Grant me the money I ask for.

Let the money flow to me.
An' it harm none, so mote it be.

Put the folded check in your purse or wallet until the money comes to you.

MONEY OWED SPELLS

William Shakespeare wrote in Hamlet, "Neither a borrower nor a lender be." Unfortunately, in this day and age, it is difficult not to be at least one of these (if not both at the same time). When money is owed either to us or from us, trying to repay the debt or asking someone to pay us back can take up so much of our time and resources. This can become frustrating and is a constant worry, especially when we don't have the money. This next set of spells is dedicated especially for this time-consuming experience of being either a lender or a borrower.

The Return to Me Spell

Here is a spell for when someone is holding on to your money. We are going to ask Pluto to help. Pluto is a rather

formidable god and a force to be reckoned with. He is the god of the underworld!

You will need a black candle and a green candle. Please do this spell inside a circle of salt; just sprinkle some salt around you, and make sure you have all you need already in the circle before you begin. Say this:

Mighty Pluto, truth and justice I seek.
Another owes me money.
Their name is [name].
Let their conscience be pricked.
Let what is rightfully mine return to me.
An' it harm none, mighty Pluto, so mote it be.

Say the spell four times over the burning candles. Afterward, give thanks to Pluto, and extinguish the candles with a candlesnuffer. Do not blow out these candles.

Wait a week and see what happens. If the person withholding your money has not been in touch, perform the spell again, but only do this spell a maximum of three times.

The Send Me the Money Spell

If someone owes you money but is not paying up, try this spell. On a piece of yellow cardstock or paper, write their name and how much they owe you. Draw a pentagram on the paper, too. Then hold the paper in your hands as you say,

> *Mighty and powerful Mercury,*
> *bring money and justice to me.*
> *Let all that I am owed come back to me.*
> *An' it harm none, so mote it be.*

Fold the paper in four and keep it with your finance information.

SAVING MONEY

If you are trying to save money but every month something happens, leaving you without anything to save, then these spells are for you.

A Nest Egg Spell

Make two holes in an egg, one at the top and one at the bottom, and blow out the yolk and whites. This can take a while, and you may need to make several attempts at it. If you prefer, you can put a small straw in the hole at the top and blow out the yolk that way.

When you have blown out the egg, wash it by running cool water through it and leave it to dry. Write on a small piece of paper how much you want your savings to grow by $1,000, $10,000…? It is entirely up to you.

When your egg is completely dry, roll up the paper and place it carefully inside the egg. If you have a garden, bury the egg outdoors. If not, get a money plant and bury the egg in its soil. As you bury it, say these words:

Little nest egg, grow for me.
Big and strong you shall be.
All my savings shall grow with money.
An' it harm none, so mote it be.

Lovingly tend to the plant and watch your nest egg grow.

The Help Me Save Money Spell

If you would like to save money but are always overdrawn by the end of the month, then this spell is for you. Anoint a silver candle with basil oil, light it, and say these words:

> *Universe, help me to save.*
> *Help me to put money away.*
> *Help me to save for a rainy day.*
> *Help me to have some money for me.*
> *An' it harm none, so mote it be.*

Do the spell for eight nights. Write out a savings plan for the next four months!

The Acorn Increase Prosperity Spell

Acorns are good for many things, including attracting a lover; they are also perfect for increasing income and prosperity. If you can, find a real acorn and spray it with gold paint (better still to collect several and spray them all gold). When they are dry, arrange them in the shape of a pentagram, or draw the pentagram on a piece of yellow cardstock or paper. You will also need some gold material—cut into five circles the size of a saucer—and some green ribbon; we are going to make little pouches.

Put an acorn on each of the five points of the pentagram. If you have more acorns, put them in the center of the pentagram. If you just have one, put it in the center. Sprinkle some saffron over the golden acorns. Light a yellow candle and say these words:

Money flow to me from every point,
north, south, east, west.
Money comes to me which way seems best.
Please, pentagram magic, blessed be.
An' it harm none, so mote it be.

Say the rhyme five times. Each time, imagine money coming to you from each point of the pentagram, like the beams of light streaking out from the candle.

Afterward, put an acorn in the center of each gold circle of material, gather it up, and tie it with the green ribbon. If you only have one acorn, that's fine; keep the gold bag near your bank details or where you keep money. If you have five acorns, put the gold pouches around your house or in the corners of your rooms. You can hang them up or hide them if you haven't yet ventured out of the broom cupboard and don't want to have to explain anything to nosey people.

The Leprechaun Money Magic Spell

Gold is revered today as much as it was in the ancient world. Gold is magical and powerful and was the object of kings and the gods. It is the color of the sun and with it comes the power of the sun. There were many magical beings whose responsibility was the protection and ownership of gold. Here in this spell, we are going to channel some leprechaun magic. These peculiar little folks of Ireland were fine crafts-men of shoes and knew a thing or two about making and saving money. They hid their pots of gold at the ends of rain-bows, although, to them, gold was not just shiny wealth, but magic in its purest form.

You may not believe that leprechauns exist, but it is what they represent that matters to us here—wealth and magic, and we want both. You will need one green candle, four gold-colored coins, some gold material cut into a circle the size of a small plate, and some black ribbon. The ribbon represents the actual pot the leprechauns kept their gold in; the pot was usually black.

Light the green candle and place the four coins around it, saying these words:

> Golden magic of leprechaun charm,
> an' it do no harm,
> magic pot of gold,
> send me the wealth of old.
> Golden magic, send wealth to me.
> Leprechaun magic, so mote it be.

Afterward, as you watch the flame, imagine your own pot of gold overflowing with money. Put the coins in the center of the circle of gold material and secure it with the black ribbon, like a pouch. Keep the gold bundle in a place where you keep your financial papers, and let the candle burn down by itself.

A Money Charm Spell

   2 cinnamon sticks

   2 bay leaves

   Some thin green ribbon

Do this spell on a Friday, as that is the night of the goddess Venus, who governs money. Make a hole in the bay leaves small enough to let the thin green ribbon go through. Tie the cinnamon sticks together with the ribbon. Thread the ribbon through the bay leaves so that the cinnamon sticks and bay leaves are together, and secure them with a bow. As you make the charm, say these words:

> *Goddess Venus, blessed be.*
> *Send your financial wisdom to me.*
> *Goddess Venus, I beseech thee.*
> *Please send money to me.*
> *An' it harm none, so mote it be.*

Hang the charm somewhere in sight, such as in the kitchen or in the room you use most. Indeed, you could make several charms and put them in every room of the house. They also make nice gifts for friends. You could arrange a money basket for a friend with the money charm, a green candle, and a golden acorn. It's always good to think of others when working with money magic.

The Dragon Gold Spell

Legend tells us that dragons loved gold! They loved gold as much as any king or god and would hoard it in great caves; woe betide the brave but annoying knight who ventured near enough to steal it.

Burn a red candle and have a piece of obsidian, which, by some people, is still called "dragon stone" as it was forged in volcanoes. Another dragon stone is septarian, which has the appearance of scales. With the obsidian or septarian near the candle, say these words:

> *Mighty dragons, lovers of gold,*
> *your strength and powers of old,*
> *help me in my quest.*
> *Fill me with your power and zest.*
> *Grant the wealth of your yellow metal,*

sweep through the centuries to me.
An' it harm none, so mote it be.

If the flame flickers, they have heard your request; do not be frightened, just embrace their magic. Keep the piece of obsidian or septarian in your purse or wallet.

DEBT SPELLS

If you find yourself in debt or having financial problems, seek professional advice. Nevertheless, here are some spells specifically written with debt in mind that focus on the most common types of debt, such as credit cards and loans.

A Credit Card Spell

This spell requires you to shift your consciousness. If you wish to be free of debt on your credit cards, try this spell. Place all your credit or store cards in a bowl. Next, take a pair of scissors, and cut all but one of them up! (If they are all maxed out, then cut every one of them up.) You do not need them, and you are trying to be debt-free. Cut each card into four pieces, and while doing so, say these words:

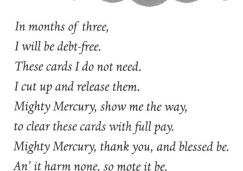

> *In months of three,*
> *I will be debt-free.*
> *These cards I do not need.*
> *I cut up and release them.*
> *Mighty Mercury, show me the way,*
> *to clear these cards with full pay.*
> *Mighty Mercury, thank you, and blessed be.*
> *An' it harm none, so mote it be.*

Set your mind to pay the cards off in three months, or you can rewrite the spell depending on how many cards you have. Just make sure the spell has eight lines, as we need the power of eight with this one.

The End My Money Woes Spell

Use a green candle and have some basil seeds nearby. You are going to plant the basil seeds and watch your money grow. Recite this over the green candle:

> *Help me, Cernunnos,*
> *save me from my money woes.*
> *Shed light on my financial strife,*

to help me find the path that is right.
Great Cernunnos, blessed be.
An' it harm none, so mote it be.

Plant the seeds in a little pot of soil and tenderly care for them. Ask Cernunnos for help with money woes often so that they become less and less.

A Goldstone Charm

This is a good spell if you have a meeting with a bank manager, an accountant, or anyone who might be able to grant you money—such as a mortgage or a loan—or help you with debt or give financial advice. You want some money luck to rub off on you.

Find a goldstone bracelet or necklace—any piece of goldstone jewelry you can wear every day. Anoint a yellow or gold candle with saffron oil. Place the goldstone jewelry around or near the candle and say these words:

My finances have run amok.
Goddess Juno, send me money luck.
Place upon this stone of gold.

Let my finances increase tenfold.
Goddess Juno, thank you, and blessed be.
An' it harm none, so mote it be.

Let the candle burn as long as you can, then extinguish it with a candlesnuffer. Wear the goldstone jewelry whenever you have an important financial meeting—before, during, and after. Take the goldstone charm off and thank it before you go to bed.

A Money Guidance Spell

If you have absolutely no idea what to do regarding money, seek professional help from a financial advisor. After, ask the gods for help and guidance. Try to do this spell on a Wednesday. Light a silver candle and recite these words:

Mighty Hermes, your guidance I need.
My money and finances are a mess.
The best course of action I know not.
Please, Hermes, show me the way,
the best paths to take for my pay.

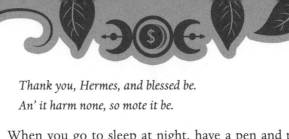

> *Thank you, Hermes, and blessed be.*
> *An' it harm none, so mote it be.*

When you go to sleep at night, have a pen and paper handy, as the answer may come to you in a dream. But the answer could come at any time, so carry a pen and paper with you always. Repeat the spell for seven nights until you have an answer. When you do, thank Hermes.

Phone Financial Success Spell

If you are waiting for a phone call regarding an important financial deal or you need to use your phone regarding any financial transaction, cast a spell on your phone to have a successful outcome (and don't forget to wear your gold-stone charm). Hold your phone between your hands like a prayer. Say,

> *Phone in my hand,*
> *grant only this.*
> *In every transaction,*
> *I will find only bliss.*

As you say these words, imagine the successful conversation and outcome in your mind's eye. You are now turning your phone into a powerful financial amulet; keep it with you wherever you go.

The Gods of the North Money Spell

In this spell, we are going to ask the Norse god Njord for help in receiving wealth. He is the god of the sea, wind, fishing, wealth, and fertility, so he really is a useful god to be aware of. Find a piece of amber, often known as "the gold of the North." Light a yellow candle and place the amber in view of the flame, saying,

> Great Njord, bestow your gifts,
> your strength, your money power, to me.
> Bless this gold of the North with riches galore.
> An' it harm none, so mote it be.

Put the piece of amber in your purse or wallet. For this spell, it is all right to blow out the candle, as Njord is also the god of the wind. Imagine the candle smoke rising through the winds to Njord, whispering your plea to him.

Amulet Infuse Spell

One of the main things that accompanies the realm of money is the amulet. Many ancient civilizations had all manner of artifacts as amulets hanging in shops or carried on their person to bring good fortune to their business or to their house and family. An amulet can be absolutely anything that you feel brings you luck in this world—including financial luck. This is a generic spell for infusing an amulet with the right intent. You can use it for money, but an amulet can be adapted for other purposes, such as love, career, or health.

If you have a favorite piece of jewelry, hold it in your hands. Burn some incense—preferably pine or oak, if you can find some.

As you hold the jewelry in your hands, infuse it with your desires. Is it meant to bring you luck with money and career when you wear it?

Holding the jewelry in your hands and thinking of these desires, say,

> *Power of the ancestors, rise.*
> *Smoke, rise to the skies.*

Release the magic to me,
power in this jewelry.

Waft the piece of jewelry several times through the burning incense smoke. Your charmed jewelry is now ready to wear to gain the desired effect you have created.

Tarot Money Luck

One of the great ways to change your luck regarding money is to use different resources, and one of the best resources is tarot. You are going to need a quartz crystal, a tarot deck (of course), and a spare notebook, though you can always use your Grimoire or Book of Shadows if you're keeping resources to a minimum.

Shuffle the deck of tarot cards, filling it with positive energy. Take the top card of the deck and place it facedown. Place the quartz crystal on top of the card and say,

Quartz crystal, with your luck so full.
Transfer some to me, please.
This tarot card shall bring good luck.
I ask of you this, so mote it be.

Keep the quartz on the card for a couple of minutes, then remove the crystal and flip the card over. Note the card and its effects in the notebook. Make sure to date the reading. If it's positive, continue reading. If not, try again tomorrow.

If your readings are negative during the next five days, start over, and always make sure to date your readings.

UNHEALTHY MONEY PROBLEMS

In our world today, it is so easy to become addicted to shopping. So many people find it all too easy to whip out their credit card and buy what they see online or in the shops, but this can have devastating effects on our lives. We start to become addicted to this behavior and find ourselves feeding huge appetites of consumption. It can get to the point where we start hoarding the products we buy, and before we know it, we are surrounded by objects and items we do not need. The closet, wardrobes, and cupboards no longer close, drawers overflow and break with the amount of rubbish stored in them, and we start to drown in our own gluttony. The next couple of spells have been devised with these modern problems in mind.

See the Squalor Spell

If you realize how you are living is wrong but are unsure as to why it's wrong, here is a spell to help you see your living environment as it is.

Closing your eyes and holding a pair of sunglasses in your hands, say,

> *Show me what others see,*
> *in all its brutal clarity.*
> *Shades of dark, see the light.*
> *Show me what can be right.*

Put the sunglasses on and open your eyes. You will see nothing wrong through them. Take them off, and, with your own eyes, see the mess around you. Look at it for some time and acknowledge that you created this mess and that you need to start clearing it. Put the sunglasses on again and say,

> *Show me what can be,*
> *when all is cleared and free.*

Open your eyes, look through the sunglasses, and see the possibility of a home free of clutter.

Friend, See the Reality Affirmation Spell

If you are a friend or family member of someone who has yet to see the folly of their ways and is basically a hoarder, you need to help them. You are going to pray to the universe to help them see the error of their ways. Have a photograph of your friend to look at, and then light one white candle on a Monday night. Meditate upon the flame for some moments before saying,

> Blessed friends, you and I.
> We may not see eye to eye.
> But you are blind and do not see,
> the squalor surrounding thee.
> Universe, I pray, give them sight,
> and help them to do what's right.

Visualize your friend suddenly realizing how they are living and clearing their mess away.

Credit Card Binding Spell

This spell is all about you facing your debt and spending; it asks you to take charge and acknowledge your habits. A credit card and a black ribbon are required for this spell. Light a black candle. Sitting down with paper and a red pen, write out how much you owe, then draw a line underneath it. After the line, write what you last spent on the credit card, the time and place of the purchase, and what it was you bought. Fold the paper and drop some black candle wax onto it to keep it shut. Begin to wrap the black ribbon around the credit card, saying these words as you do so:

> *Into the black you must go.*
> *No more spending woe.*
> *I bind this card, no more to spend.*
> *This debt I owe must end.*

Wrap the card and folded paper together with what's left of the ribbon and seal with black candle wax once more. As you do this, say,

I bind this card with this seal, never to break.
The spending is finished, never more to take.

When the wax is completely dry, place the bound card and paper somewhere safe and out of your way for at least twelve months, and never break the seal until the debt has been paid.

Declutter the House Spell

This is quite a tough spell as it requires total honesty. You have to be willing and ruthless in letting go most of what you have accumulated over the time you have been hoarding. For many people who are suffering with hoarding tendencies, this is a shock to the system, but you have to start somewhere. Depending on the severity of the hoarding, start in one room or drawer, and work your way through the house. Don't try to tackle it all at once as you will soon give up.

In the room you want to start on first, stand in the middle of it and look around. In your mind, see three piles of clothes, shoes, or whatever objects you hoard. One pile is to sell, one pile is for charity, and one pile is to give away to friends and family. At this point, there is no pile for you to keep, so don't try sneaking it in! You will only end up keeping everything.

In the room, arms by your sides and palms facing outward, say,

> *Help me see space.*
> *Here, in this place.*
> *No more the catastrophe,*
> *of my spending spree.*
> *Go now from this place.*
> *Eradicate all before my face.*

Be strong and ruthless. Work for at least an hour on this, and don't stop until you can see the space. Have a friend help you, and as soon as you have cleared a space, have your friend put the items in garbage bags, ready to be taken to their next place. Have your friend start moving the bags out into their car so the objects are out of your sight completely, and let them go that very day.

The Lucky Bag Spell

There are times when we need a little extra support with finances, and so let us finish this section with a delightfully positive spell on enticing money to flow to us instead of from us.

On a small piece of paper, write out your intention with a green pen. Mix a pinch of allspice and a pinch of nutmeg with a drop of water. Then, with your index finger, create a streak on the back of the paper, and say,

> *This substance of nature,*
> *bound this parchment.*
> *My command upon written luck, I implore.*
> *Universe, please give me more.*

Roll up the paper like a little scroll and tie it with a green ribbon. Place it in a small green bag. Also, place a piece of your jewelry in the bag along with a stone, preferably moss agate.

Tie your bag and say,

> *My will be done; universe, hear my plea.*
> *An' it harm none, so mote it be.*

Place the bag where you keep your money paperwork, such as near checkbooks and bank statements, or hang it where you make money if you work in a shop or on a computer (if the boss will allow it).

※

There are many areas where money is a necessity to survive, yet does one individual need so much to be happy? We can be happy and content with just the basics—many people throughout this world survive on a lot less than we have in the West.

You can, of course, change the wording of any spell to suit your own particular situation; just remember the correspondences, which were discussed at the beginning of this chapter. Next, we shall look at the subject of careers, which can also be related to financial rewards. The two are often combined with great effect.

MORE MONEY CORRESPONDENCES

Here is a list of additional resources you can use as substitutions in the money spells. You can also use these correspondences to create your own money spells to fit your own situation. All the resources listed here have their harmonics in tune with the subject of money and finance.

Herbs and Fruit

Allspice is a good spice for money and wealth spells (and for healing). It makes a good incense.

Anise hyssop leaves have antibacterial properties and also make a refreshing tea with a minty flavor.

Cinnamon has so many wondrous uses; it is a staple in any witch's kitchen.

Cloves are wonderful, but do not put the actual cloves into candles as they can ignite and combust. If you would like to put the scent into a candle, use the oil instead.

Pomegranate is a great fruit for fertility and for money.

Thyme is an antiseptic, antibacterial, and antifungal herb. A truly wonderful plant for anything and everything, though it's not to be used during pregnancy as it is a uterine stimulant.

Crystals

Citrine has always been a great stone throughout history. In many countries, merchants would carry a piece in their money boxes, thus it became known as the "merchant's stone."

Emerald is great for legal or business matters, so carry a piece when seeing the bank manager.

Peridot is a good stone for helping you decide your destiny.

Sapphire is the stone of wisdom, loyalty, and truth.

Turquoise is the traveler's stone.

Essential Oils

Honeysuckle is a beautifully smelling oil—very sensual, but also very positive when used in money spells.

Nutmeg oil should always be used sparingly as it does have a toxic compound, which can cause hallucinations and convulsions—please be careful with this.

Oak moss oil blends well with orange oil and can be used as an antiseptic.

Saffron oil is fantastic for its digestive properties; it also improves circulation and reduces high blood pressure. It is also the richest known source of vitamin B_2.

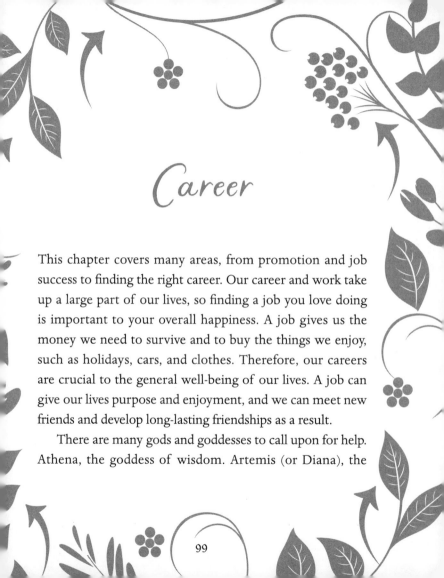

Career

This chapter covers many areas, from promotion and job success to finding the right career. Our career and work take up a large part of our lives, so finding a job you love doing is important to your overall happiness. A job gives us the money we need to survive and to buy the things we enjoy, such as holidays, cars, and clothes. Therefore, our careers are crucial to the general well-being of our lives. A job can give our lives purpose and enjoyment, and we can meet new friends and develop long-lasting friendships as a result.

There are many gods and goddesses to call upon for help. Athena, the goddess of wisdom. Artemis (or Diana), the

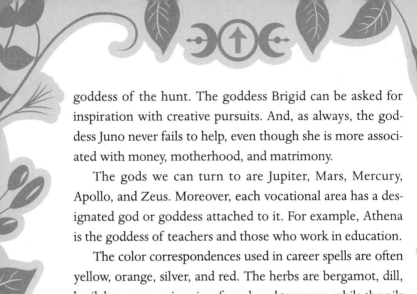

goddess of the hunt. The goddess Brigid can be asked for inspiration with creative pursuits. And, as always, the goddess Juno never fails to help, even though she is more associated with money, motherhood, and matrimony.

The gods we can turn to are Jupiter, Mars, Mercury, Apollo, and Zeus. Moreover, each vocational area has a designated god or goddess attached to it. For example, Athena is the goddess of teachers and those who work in education.

The color correspondences used in career spells are often yellow, orange, silver, and red. The herbs are bergamot, dill, basil, lemongrass, jasmine, fennel, and tarragon, while the oils are pine, rosemary, frankincense, and sandalwood. The number to use here is three, as three is the number of sociability—we do need to get along with others in our work. It is also the number that represents the past, present, and future. Three also represents artistic expression, and all of us, no matter how mundane our jobs are, can find some creativity in them.

QUICK REFERENCE
CORRESPONDENCE CHART

Colors	orange and yellow
Crystals	citrine
Flower	jasmine
Incense	pine
Oil	rosemary
Day	Thursday or Sunday
Deities	Mars
Planet	Jupiter
Number	3

CAREER PLANNING

I am sure we have all experienced a career day at school or college, wherein we are expected to say what our chosen career path is when we are still teenagers. You are lucky if you know what you want to do at sixteen or eighteen. However, some of us still have no idea as we approach our fifties! The next couple of spells are designed to help you find your heart's desire—or at least point you in the right direction of your soul's path.

Heart's Desire Charm

If you are unsure of what you want to do for your career, buy a heart-shaped pendant, brooch, or piece of jewelry. Hold it in your hands and concentrate. Then say,

> *Grant me my heart's desire.*
> *Whatever that may be.*
> *An' it harm none, so mote it be.*

Write out several jobs or careers that you may like to do, such as nurse, teacher, chef, and so on. Then, holding your heart jewelry, move it over the list, keeping your eyes closed until you feel a sort of tingle. It can feel like pins and needles in your fingers or even a little shock. Open your eyes to see which career you should be studying or going for.

Wear your piece of heart jewelry whenever you feel you are waning from your true purpose in life.

Career Clarity Spell

This is a spell to clarify which direction you should follow for satisfaction in your work. Light a yellow candle anointed with frankincense and sandalwood oil. Say these words:

> My life is hard decisions abound.
> Show me the way that I can see,
> help me to know clarity.
> Wheel of life, round and round,
> am I up, or am I down?
> So much strife in work have I,
> no balance, no life, constant fight.
> Please, Mother Juno, help,
> guide me to restore balance,
> let me be strong to take a chance.
> An' it harm none, so mote it be.

Keep a pen and paper with you, or, better still, your own Book of Shadows. The answer to your career clarity will be shown to you within the next month. Look for the signs; they may appear in different forms, but trust your instincts. You will know what is right and wrong in your working life and how to resolve it.

The CV/Resume Blast Spell

When you know the job you want, you must put in the effort to get it. One thing you need is a CV that will make bosses hire you on the spot. First, research the most up-to-date CVs on the internet and spend a good hour or more working on yours. After, as you hold the CV in your hands, recite these words:

> *I work on my CV for hours.*
> *Grant me success and power.*
> *Above the rest will be my CV.*
> *An' it harm none, so mote it be.*

After you have completed the spell and written your CV, put it in a drawer for an ample time and forget about it. Then, take it out and look at it again. Trust your instincts about any changes that need to be made until you are ready to send it away to your prospective employers.

An Interview Charm Spell

When you are going to an interview, make sure you wear something you feel confident in, and, if you can, wear a piece of turquoise jewelry or carry a piece in your pocket. Turquoise is great for protection, but it is also a good luck stone. It enhances communication and inspiration, which are certainly needed in some of today's challenging job interviews. Do this spell on a Wednesday. Hold the turquoise in your hand as you say,

> Mighty Mercury, quick and wise,
> help me to be the best surprise.
> The interviewers will hire me on the spot.
> They will know I am right for the job.
> Mighty Mercury, I will be the best interviewee.
> An' it harm none, so mote it be.

New Moon New Job Spell

Suppose you now have a nice new job—well done. Write down your goals for the new job, both personal and professional. Decide ten goals or targets for the coming year (or for however long the contract lasts). Anoint a yellow candle with lemongrass and bergamot. On the night of a new moon, light the candle; then, holding your ten goals in your hand, say these words:

> *Father Jupiter, blessed be,*
> *a new job have I.*
> *Grant me success in goals of ten,*
> *help me prove my worth and then,*
> *victorious I shall be.*
> *An' it harm none, so mote it be.*

Meditate on your goals for a while and keep the candle burning for as long as you can before extinguishing it or letting it burn itself out.

CAREER PROBLEMS

Most of us in this world have to work. We work for many reasons, but primarily to keep a roof over our heads, put food on the table, and provide for our families. We work because we need to survive. Though there are people who also view work as their life, and if this is the case, good luck to them.

Although we spend a vast amount of time at work, it may not be so happy due to people who can be negative. These people can make work unbearable for us. If you are having problems, please speak to your line manager regarding them, if possible.

A Forgiveness at Work Spell

Sometimes in our place of work, we encounter enemies whom we need to forgive in order to move on. Although it is often difficult to forget things, we can always try to forgive and go forward in the knowledge that we tried.

Anoint an orange candle with frankincense and rosemary essential oils. Write the name of the person you need

to forgive on a piece of red paper. Light the candle and focus on the name as you say these words:

> *Universe, hear my plea.*
> *From anger toward [name], I am free.*
> *Let me forgive [name],*
> *for all the pain they sent me.*
> *An' it harm none, so mote it be.*

Afterward, burn the paper and wash the burned pieces away with holy water. You might do this spell outside so you can wash everything away easily. Remember, though, to keep the candle away from the water!

Negative Office Spell

Despite your best intentions, not everyone you work with will like you. Moreover, you might be able to feel the negative office vibes straight away, whether directed at you or not. One way to protect yourself is to imagine a mirrored cloak around you so that whatever comes your way is bounced right back to the sender.

There are other ways we can counteract negative office energy, such as performing this spell. Find yourself some smoky quartz—either jewelry or simply a small piece. Nowadays, in many New Age shops, you can find smoky quartz angels that can sit on your desk. This is a stone that can help heal and absorb negative energies. However, we need to give it some power before we take it into work. In the light of a silver candle, rub some frankincense oil onto the smoky quartz as you recite these words:

Smoky quartz, powers be.
Absorb the painful negativity,
so that my place of work will be light and free.
An' it harm none, so mote it be.

Take the smoky quartz with you to work and leave it there all week. At the end of the week, take it home and soak it in some salt water overnight. Do the ritual again over the weekend to be ready for the next work week. Do this as often as you need to.

Protection and Clearing Spell

This is a good spell to protect you at work or to "clear the air." Make some holy water: magic sea salt and water with three drops of frankincense oil. Shake it up and put it into a spray bottle. Before anyone gets into your place of work—or if you are the last to leave—spray around the office or wherever you are for the majority of time. Hold an obsidian crystal in your hand as you do so, and say,

> *Circle of protection, I invoke thee.*
> *Let me be safe and free,*
> *encased within your loving embrace,*
> *forever protected from those in this place.*
> *An' it harm none, so mote it be.*

Obsidian is a good stone to have at work as it sends negative thoughts on their way. However, you can also do this spell at home if you wish, covering yourself with protection in case you are confronted with something hurtful. Just change the spell to your individual situation.

A Gossipmonger Spell

The gossip is a danger to all who come into contact with them. They can and will gossip about anything and everything. News is strange with the gossip as it can begin with a truth, which then gets completely distorted.

This is a spell, basically, to send all the negativity back to the gossipmongers. You could perform this at work in the bathroom or anywhere you could be alone for five minutes. Imagine the person before you and visualize their face, then think of a mirror surrounding you. See their gossip and lies coming toward you like arrows that bounce off the mirror and straight back to them, then say,

> *Loose lips sink ships, your lies hurt many.*
> *Return now to your venom and deceit.*
> *Friends at work, you will not have any.*
> *Swallow your gossip and lies, they are not sweet.*
> *Truth shall prevail and throw you from your liars' seat.*

New Job, Hate It Spell

Oh dear! Sometimes, regardless of our best intentions, the new job we strove for is not what we imagined. We find out the hard way that the grass is not greener on the other side. What can we do? Buy a jasmine plant to keep indoors. Write down what is wrong with the job and what you need to change about it, if it can indeed be changed. Then say these words over the plant:

> *Lady Brigid, goddess of inspirations,*
> *help me please.*
> *A career mistake I have made.*
> *Show me the right path in months of three.*
> *An' it harm none, so mote it be.*

When the flowers bloom on the plant, a new path, such as a new job or an invitation to try something new with your career, will present itself to you—perhaps sooner than three months.

SPELLS FOR SPECIFIC PROFESSIONS

Here is a selection of spells with specific professions in mind. There are many careers in one area. For example, if you work in any area to do with the earth, such as gardening, landscaping, or even forestry, then this horticulture spell is for you. Alternatively, there are correspondences at the end of this chapter that can be used to write your own spell specific to your situation and career.

A Horticulture Spell

If you work in horticulture and have some problems with the plants, there are many appropriate spells, from blessing the soil or plants to creating magical compost.

There are two crystals that are particularly good to work with in a horticultural setting. The first is moonstone, which helps gardeners get their green fingers creating magic again. The other is malachite, which helps plants bloom longer. We also use the fresh herbs tarragon and fennel. Place the stones (you can use both malachite and moonstone) atop the fresh herbs. Say these words:

> *Light and dark, black and white,*
> *let my garden bloom big and bright.*
> *Flowers and plants, large and small,*
> *blessed be to one and all.*

Carry the stones in your pocket when you go to work and put the herbs in the garden to heal the soil.

A Legal Spell

If you are a lawyer or work in a legal setting, the crystal for you is bloodstone. Jokes aside, this is a very powerful stone and often brings the owner victory in whatever dealings they have.

Light a red candle and say these words over the bloodstone on a Tuesday:

> *Hear me, Mars, hear me, Mars,*
> *victory I do seek.*
> *In all my work, I beseech thee,*
> *let me win, always victory.*
> *An' it harm none, so mote it be.*

Wear or keep the stone on your person in all your business dealings.

A Spell for Business—The Good Luck Besom

This is a good luck charm to hang above the door of your business or workplace or home office. You are going to make a small besom, or broom.

Go out for a walk in the park or in the woods and collect several fallen twigs. They only need to be about ten to fifteen centimeters long, with one longer and thicker. This will be the central twig that the others are attached to. Bring all the small twigs together and attach them around the central twig at one end, securing them with an elastic band. Tie a red ribbon around the elastic band to hide it. If you can, attach a little bell to the ribbon and also an acorn, painted gold.

> *Little good luck witch, riding this broom,*
> *luck and prosperity, you bring to this room.*
> *Grant success in all that I do.*
> *Little besom, blessed be.*

An' it harm none, for now and evermore,
So mote it be.

Hang the besom up above a door and occasionally dress it with fennel, dill, rosemary, or jasmine flowers.

A *Spell for Health Professionals*

Everybody, no matter their role in life, needs a little boost. Health professionals and those who work in the caring professions also need a little help themselves now and again. This is a spell especially written for those who work in that arena. We shall ask Apollo for his help, as he is one of the gods of medicine. He is also the sun god, and we need his golden light of healing and warmth in our caring work.

Anoint or make a yellow candle with jasmine and rosemary oils. If making the candle, put in three drops of each oil. Recite this spell over the light of the candle:

Mighty Apollo, gracious golden sun,
help the healing ones,
they who care for those in pain and need.
Spread your warmth and care to them.

May your strength power their pursuits.
For now and evermore, blessed be.
An' it harm none, so mote it be.

Keep the candle burning as long as possible and meditate awhile for all those who help the sick and needy.

Retail Charm Spell

If you work in the retail sector, things may have been difficult in recent years given the popularity of online shopping. Create a retail charm to hang in your shop or retail business.

You will need red ribbon, a golden acorn, a coin, and a piece of citrine. Drill a little hole in the citrine, the coin, and the acorn (if it is a real one. Better still, a golden acorn charm will usually have a loop on it already). Thread the three charms onto the red ribbon and secure them with a knot at both ends so they don't fall down the ribbon. If you are unable to drill holes in the items, place the acorn, coin, and citrine in a small red satin or silk bag and secure it with a red ribbon. Hang your charm in your shop or place of work, saying these words:

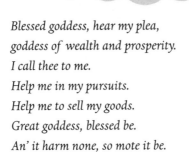

Blessed goddess, hear my plea,
goddess of wealth and prosperity.
I call thee to me.
Help me in my pursuits.
Help me to sell my goods.
Great goddess, blessed be.
An' it harm none, so mote it be.

It would also be wise to put an image of an elephant or owl in your shop, or any other symbols of prosperity you feel akin to.

CAREER BOOST

In our chosen careers, we all could do with a little boost—whether a promotion, a pay raise, or just an acknowledgment for hard work. The next couple of spells have been designed to help you get that promotion or recognition. They also cover boosting your career prospects when confronted with external influences, such as a recession or trouble communicating with a boss.

A Promotion Spell

You are doing a great job at work and really want that promotion. Show off your power and your light. Light an anointed yellow candle. Write your prospective job on a piece of yellow cardstock or paper and drop three drops of bergamot oil onto it as you recite these words:

> *Father Jupiter, strong and bright,*
> *let me show these bosses my might.*
> *For the promotion, I am right.*
> *Father Jupiter, blessed be.*
> *An' none shall it harm.*
> *So mote it be.*

Afterward, fold up the paper three times and keep it in your drawer until you achieve your promotion. Then give thanks and rip the card up three times before throwing it away.

The Beat the Recession Spell

If you can have a plant in your place of work, buy a marigold or rosemary plant to keep there. Before taking the plant to work, say these words over it:

Blessed Juno, in times of strife,
let this plant help in my fight.
Recession from these doors be gone.
Blessed Juno, an' it harm none,
So mote it be.

Take the plant into work and take care of it lovingly.

A Better Communication Spell

In our working lives, there are often times when we wish we hadn't said something. At other times, we often have the answer, but we are afraid to speak up. This spell is basically a confidence spell, which I have used specifically for those taking exams. However, here, we shall concentrate on communication, particularly in relation to work.

The stone that is useful here is kunzite, which has excellent communication attributes. A piece of jade is also particularly good as a wisdom-bearing stone. We want to concentrate on opening the throat (or fifth) chakra, the link between ourselves and the world around us. It is the chakra connected with communication and self-expression. Any stone of blue or green color will help open this chakra up, so sapphire, aquamarine, and turquoise are also good here.

Light a silver candle and hold your chosen stone in your hands. Imagine the light of the candle streaming into your throat, enhanced by the stone. Imagine a blockage in your throat being cleared and a pathway of blue light reflecting back into the silver candle. Start to whisper,

> Let me speak confidently.
> Blessed all, so mote it be.

Repeat this over and over again, getting louder each time until at last you say the words confidently and loudly. Take the stone or jewelry with you when you go to work.

The Candle and Needle Success Spell

This time-honored candle and needle spell has been specially formulated with your career success in mind. Anoint an orange candle with jasmine, lemongrass, and rosemary oils. Do this spell every night for a week, starting on a Thursday. Stick a needle into the candle (you can choose where on the candle you want to stick the needle). When the flame burns down to the needle, the spell takes effect.

> *Success I seek in all my business.*
> *Business, success, victory.*
> *An' it harm none, so mote it be.*

Light the candle as you say these words and let the candle burn down to the needle, then extinguish it. Move the needle down a little farther each day you do the spell, and repeat it for the following seven nights until the candle finishes.

Hard Luck Spell

At certain times in our lives, everything just seems to go against us, and nothing we do seems to go right, especially in our careers. Ask the universe for a realignment.

Stick a needle in one white candle and one black candle, then light both candles for seven nights. Each time the candle burns down to the needle, blow out the candle. Lower the needle every night.

As you light the candles each night, say these words:

Universe, hear my plea.
Send balance back to me.
I have nothing but bad luck.
Everything in my life runs amok.
Upon this rising smoke, hear me.
An' it harm none, so mote it be.

Blow out the candle and watch the rising smoke carrying your intentions toward the universe.

Try It Spell

At work, new ideas and concepts come all the time. Just when you finish one goal, a new one has been set. This fast-paced atmosphere of constant change can make many nervous, and sometimes our fears keep us back from trying new things. Do not let fear stop you from doing something you've always wanted to do. Be brave and go forward.

On a Tuesday night, light a red candle and write down what it is you want to do. Then say,

> *This is who I am.*
> *This is who I want to be.*
> *Fear, stay away from me.*

Take some moments to look into the flame and focus on your goal before blowing out the candle.

Destiny Spell

Imagine what you would like your life to be like, then light a gold candle. Say these words three times over the candle:

> *Blessed be to you, goddesses of fate.*
> *Spin me strength, health, and love.*
> *Be merciful with me and mine.*
> *By your powers of destiny, your powers divine.*
> *Be gentle with my life, be tender with my fate.*
> *Goddesses of past, present, and future, blessed be.*
> *An' it harm none, so mote it be.*

Dream Spell

Everyone has dreams and ambition. As a child, you may have dreamed of doing something great one day. As a young person going through school, college, or university, you had a desire to do something—or maybe education and going back to school is your dream.

The following spell requires a photo of you as a child, one pink candle and one yellow candle, paper, and a blue pen. On a Wednesday night, light the candles and place the photo between them. Stare at the photo and remember what you were like as a child. Remember the dreams you had: What did you always want to be? What filled your heart with excitement? When you are ready, write the answers to these questions: What did you want to do when you grew up? What was your favorite toy? What was your favorite game to play as a child? What was your favorite subject at school? Did you prefer working alone or in a group? Keep writing. Let the memories of all the dreams you had flow out from you. Then say,

> *Staring at this face, I see the dreams I once had.*
> *Let me make those dreams a reality now, in this place.*

Fold the paper around the photo and keep them in a safe place. Every day, begin to work toward your dream, no matter

how small. Does it involve going back to school? Do you need to retrain, move, dress differently, or go on a diet? Your dreams can be anything, so don't hold back. This is entirely for you now, so let go and express your thoughts.

What's Wrong with My Career Divination

The alarm goes off on that dreaded Monday morning, and you want to go back to sleep. You hate your job, and you hate everything and everyone connected to it. What can you do? Ask yourself, is your biggest nightmare the place you are working in, or the people you are working with?

We work not only for money, but to acquire a certain lifestyle and a sense of belonging—and also to be part of something meaningful. Ideally, work brings pride in a job well-done, but there can be a huge cost to us. Job dissatisfaction can manifest itself as tedium or stress. You might think you are not on top of your workload and responsibilities. You may also feel that the people around you are not pulling their weight, or you are not sufficiently appreciated, or you are never going to get ahead as your boss does not want to promote you because you do such a good job in your current position.

As you travel to work in the morning, look up to the sky. To the first cloud you see, say under your breath,

Is it the job, or is it me?
Send me a sign of clarity.

By the end of the day, you should have your answer. If not, repeat the spell until you get a sign from the universe, which may come as a subtle email, a phone call from the boss, or a conversation with someone about a job role.

EDUCATION

Education is very important in gaining the right qualifications to get the job you want. These next spells have been designed specifically with education in mind. These education spells can also be applied to training in a work setting and apprenticeships, not just to school and college.

An Exam Confidence Spell

Exams can be horrible, and, predominantly, it is the young who go through them. So much stress is put upon them, with so many hopes and dreams for the desired outcome. Thyme was used in ancient times to encourage bravery, so you could use it in food for those taking exams.

Perform this spell on a Wednesday. Gather thyme, lavender, oregano, and mint. Write out this spell and say these words:

> *Ancestors of my family,*
> *help my child in the days ahead.*
> *They worry, and their exams are a dread.*
> *Let them be brave and true.*
> *Let the answers come through.*
> *Let their pen answer wisely.*
> *An' it harm none, so mote it be.*

Light a silver candle and sprinkle the herbs over the spell you have written down. Roll up the paper with the herbs inside and secure it with some blue ribbon so that it looks like a scroll. Keep it in a safe place. When the results come through, give thanks to your ancestors, then burn the scroll and bury the remains in a garden.

The Pegasus Education Spell

There is an elemental that you can ask for help regarding education and any work where you need inspiration. In the ancient world, any animal or being who is given wings has a connection with the spirit world, either by virtue of being a messenger between heaven and earth, such as angels, or because they are some form of deity. The god Hermes has a wonderful pair of winged sandals, and he was the messenger of the gods.

Wings themselves are symbols of knowledge and enlightenment—not to mention the freedom they can bring. And because of this, Pegasus represents knowledge and is the overseer of education.

Here is a spell for help with exams and for inspiration. Light a white candle and, if you have one, hold a white feather in your hands as you say these words:

> *Blessed Pegasus, mighty and strong,*
> *let my answers be right, not wrong.*

Give me inspiration in my answers,
let my dreams and creativity soar,
give me insight once more.
Blessed Pegasus, so mote it be.

The correspondence to use with Pegasus energy is a clear quartz crystal. This amazing crystal can be used for all purposes, but particularly for expanding communication and knowledge with angels and the universe, which is what Pegasus represents. Clear quartz is everything that Pegasus is, and it can heal and reenergize the body.

Use the energy of Pegasus when you need to boost your output or you have an important exam or job interview. Pegasus embodies adventure and bravery, so imagine him when you are confronted with a new idea and rise to the challenge, allowing Pegasus to take you there.

❦

The subject of career is huge, and we spend most of our waking hours at work, so why not be doing something you love. Confucius said, "If you find a job you love to do, you never work a day in your life." And there is some truth in

that, but sometimes jobs come to us accidently or miracu-
lously, and we then realize what we were always meant to
be doing.

MORE CAREER CORRESPONDENCES

Here is a list of additional resources you can use as substitutions in the career spells. You can also use these correspondences to create your own career spells to fit your own
situation, as all the resources listed here have their harmonics in tune with the subject of career and education.

Herbs and Trees

Chamomile is a staple herb than can be used for so much,
from teas to oils and cosmetics.

Comfrey is very good for skin complaints, such as bruises, var-
icose veins, and inflamed muscles.

Elder tree is sacred to hedgewitches, so never on any occasion
destroy one. The flowers and fruit are so beneficial for us,
with medicinal, culinary, cosmetic, and household uses.

Mint is a fantastic herb for teas and essential oil; it is also an
insect repellent.

Oregano or *wild marjoram* is another wonderful general-purpose herb. A word of warning, though: marjoram is not to be used during pregnancy—either in medicinal doses or as an essential oil—as it is a uterine stimulant.

Crystals

Amazonite is a great stone for self-expression, but be careful if you're in an argument with your boss! It can give you strength when making tough decisions.

Amber, or "gold of the North," is a wonderfully calming yet strong stone that reinforces your confidence when going into battle, as it were.

Aventurine is a lovely stone for the heart, so it's good for friendship and for eliminating anger. Very useful in legal matters.

Goldstone is a great stone for success, prosperity, and getting your wish granted.

Essential Oils

Jasmine oil is great for depression and fatigue; a very feminine oil.

Marigold or *calendula oil* has anti-inflammatory and antiseptic properties and is also antibacterial and antifungal; a truly magnificent plant. It can be made into an infusion by steeping the petals in warm vegetable oil.

Orange oil is a true all-rounder as it brings peace and calm to the body and mind while gently lifting the spirit.

Woodruff oil promotes harmony and psychic awareness.

Home and Hearth

In the home, we find family, which includes not only the people we traditionally find—such as parents and siblings—but also friends and pets. There are many spells for issues from fertility to protecting the home—not to mention finding a new home and moving. Some are very ancient. The witch's protection jar for the family home is probably among the oldest of spells that have survived. Herbs were hung at the doors to ward off evil spirits, and in later years, the

QUICK REFERENCE
CORRESPONDENCE CHART

Colors	silver and gold
Crystals	quartz
Flower	Californian poppy
Incense	lily
Oil	lavendar
Day	Tuesday and Sunday
Deities	Hestia
Planet	sun
Numbers	4

horseshoe also came to represent a force of goodwill for the owner of the house.

There are many gods and goddesses of hearth and home. One to be called upon is Hestia, or her Roman equivalent, Vesta. The hearth, or the eternal flame, is her symbol. The kitchen is, of course, sacred to her, and in ancient times, the fire of the home was never allowed to go out. In Norse religion, the goddess Frigg is patron of the home, being the wife of Odin. The English word *Friday* comes from the Anglo-Saxon version of her name, Frigge; therefore, Friday is a good day for calling upon her. The other goddess to call upon is Juno, the patron of motherhood; you can call upon her if a problem involves children.

In ancient Rome, lares or familiars were called upon in household matters, and homes had altars to the family guardians. The lares are often depicted as males in tunics with garlands adorning their heads.

The colors corresponding to family are gold, silver, dark rose, lavender, black, and brown. The oils we can use are lavender, iris, lily, and peony, among others. Flowers and herbs to use are angelica, hollyhock, Californian poppy, and angel's trumpet. However, do not ingest or make oils with these, as they are highly toxic; they are only for decorative purposes and for representing a specific god or goddess.

The number four is the number for practicality and loyalty. Here also in the family subject, friends and pets make an appearance. In many cases, close friends become more like family to us through time, and pets are like the brothers and sisters we always wanted. The feeling of grief and loss when we lose a pet is the same as when we lose a close relative and loved one.

HOME

The home is not just bricks and mortar; it represents so much more. It's where we can relax, cook, entertain, and be ourselves. In this section, you can find spells on choosing the right home to live in and protecting your home.

The Witch's Protection Jar Spell

The witch's jars and bottles were once thought to be solely used for cursing and hexing, but more often they were used for protection. They can still be used for the protection of the house and all those within. Many jars in the old days would have had nails in them, because nails were made of iron. Iron is a highly regarded metal for getting rid of spirits, and it can ward off evil.

Also in the bottles, one would find pieces of fingernails or hair—the witch giving something of herself to the universe for protecting the house. This is a similar idea to money bag spells of yore, where a piece of oneself was given freely for the spell to take effect. We are going to make a house protection bottle, but not with our nails or hair (unless you want to).

1 clove of garlic

1 bay leaf

1 basil leaf

1 teaspoon of dillseeds

1 sage leaf

1 star anise

1 teaspoon of black pepper

1 teaspoon of fennel

1 teaspoon of vervain

1 tablespoon of magic sea salt

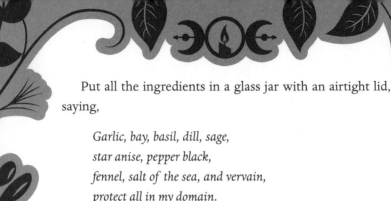

Put all the ingredients in a glass jar with an airtight lid, saying,

> *Garlic, bay, basil, dill, sage,*
> *star anise, pepper black,*
> *fennel, salt of the sea, and vervain,*
> *protect all in my domain.*
> *Salt and herbs, ten times ten,*
> *guard now and evermore my den.*
> *It is done, an' it harm none.*
> *Blessed be, so mote it be.*

Ideally, the jar would have been bricked up while the house was being built, but you can plant it somewhere in the house, such as under a floorboard or under the stairs. Failing that, you could always bury it in the bottom of a large plant pot and keep it by the door; just remember, when you leave the house, the plant and jar need to stay in the house, as the protection is for the house and all therein, not necessarily just for you.

A Home Protection Potion

4 cups of water

1 teaspoon of vervain

1 teaspoon of sea salt

1 teaspoon each of frankincense and myrrh

1 pinch of wolfsbane

Simmer the ingredients over a low flame for fifteen minutes, then let the potion cool and put it into a jar. Sprinkle this potion whenever and wherever protection is needed—for example, at the door and windows as a psychic sealant.

A Protection for the Home Spell

Another form of protection for the home can be a lion! A real one may not be practical, but symbolically the lion is regarded as regal and fearless, ruled by the sun, and having great power. Lions are known to drive away evil spirits, so lions are often guardians of sacred places and will not allow any harmful force to enter the area they are asked to protect.

Use a picture or ornament of a lion. Light a yellow candle and say over the lion,

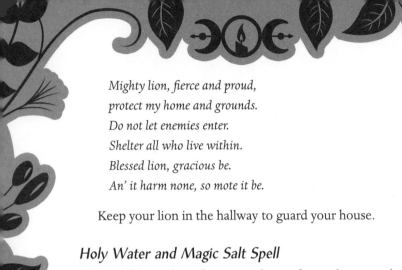

Mighty lion, fierce and proud,
protect my home and grounds.
Do not let enemies enter.
Shelter all who live within.
Blessed lion, gracious be.
An' it harm none, so mote it be.

Keep your lion in the hallway to guard your house.

Holy Water and Magic Salt Spell

This spell is to clear the atmosphere of your home and to cast a protective spell around the house. Put four table-spoonfuls of your magic sea salt in a spray bottle with four hundred milliliters (¾ pint) of water and four drops of laven-der oil. Shake it all up in the bottle and spray it around the house, going from room to room as you might with a sage stick. We are clearing the air and creating a peaceful atmo-sphere in the house. Say these words as you do so:

Blessed be to one and all in my home.
Let fighting and worry be gone.
Let love, light, and peace,

forever be in my home.
An' it harm none, so mote is be.

You can do this spell every month or every time there is a festival of the year. A list of festivals and their corresponding spells is given later.

Find Your Ideal Home Spell

Look through magazines and adverts to find pictures of the home you would like to live in. Think about the rooms and how they look, the garden, the kitchen, the bathroom, and the number of bedrooms. Then stick the pictures on a piece of cardstock and sprinkle your magic salt over them. Using your index finger, write *home* in the salt.

This house is mine.
I will find it in time.
Bring it to me and all I see.

Afterward, hang the picture of your ideal home in a place where you will see it every day.

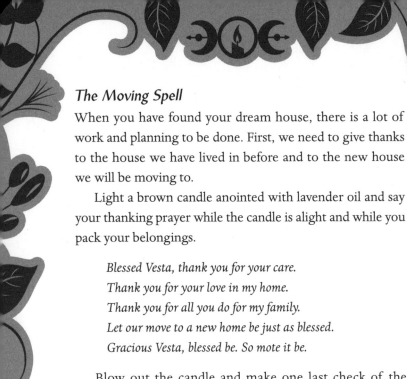

The Moving Spell

When you have found your dream house, there is a lot of work and planning to be done. First, we need to give thanks to the house we have lived in before and to the new house we will be moving to.

Light a brown candle anointed with lavender oil and say your thanking prayer while the candle is alight and while you pack your belongings.

> *Blessed Vesta, thank you for your care.*
> *Thank you for your love in my home.*
> *Thank you for all you do for my family.*
> *Let our move to a new home be just as blessed.*
> *Gracious Vesta, blessed be. So mote it be.*

Blow out the candle and make one last check of the house. Go from room to room, saying thank you in each, before leaving. Good luck in your new home.

FAMILY

Our families are so varied today; they can be large or small. They can have a single parent, or two, or three, or even none. We may have lost loved ones; we may not speak to family members, or we may view our friends as family. Here are a few spells for families, from fertility spells to gratitude spells for family members.

Fertility Spells

There are many old customs and traditions concerning fertility. One of them was to keep a cucumber in the bedroom, which was believed to increase fertility. For a man to increase his virility, it was said that he needed to eat an egg every day for forty days. However, to counteract this, there was another saying: simply, "egg-bound!" Another ancient English fertility spell for men has to do with walnuts and chestnuts, surprise surprise ...

    1 pinch of jasmine
    1 pinch of dried oak leaf

1 pinch of rose petals
1 pinch of marjoram

Mix the ingredients together with a pestle and mortar. Grind the mixture into a fine powder and sprinkle it under the bed. With regard to the oak leaf, do not pull the leaf off a tree. Look on the ground, as nature will have supplied one for you.

A Male Fertility Spell
Steep five chestnuts in a pot of water for five hours. Strain and bury the nuts outside, but keep the water and add it to your bath.

Another Male Fertility Spell
This is a more modern version of the previous spell.

4 walnuts in their shells
4 walnuts without their shells
4 chestnuts
1 bowl of water

Put all the ingredients in the water and leave them for one night in the light of a full moon. While in the moonlight, say these words over the water:

> *Father Jupiter, blessed be.*
> *Grant me a healthy baby.*
> *Help me grow a loving family.*
> *An' it harm none, so mote it be.*

In the morning, bury the nuts and keep the water to use in your bath.

A Female Fertility Spell

Rub iris or lavender oil onto a moonstone as you say these words. Keep the moonstone near your bed, and have some fresh peony flowers in your bedroom, too, if possible. Allow three months for this spell. If you have not conceived by then, repeat the spell.

> *Goddess Juno, mother of all,*
> *I ask you to help me.*
> *Help me to conceive.*

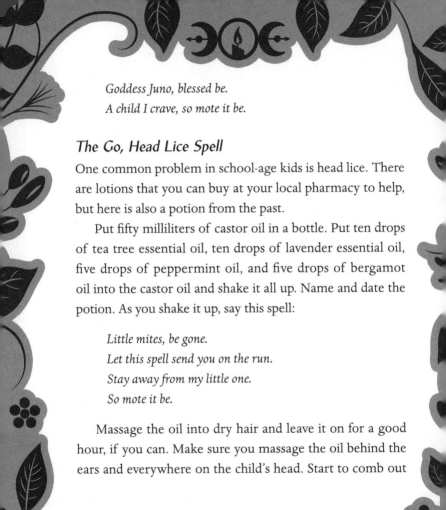

Goddess Juno, blessed be.
A child I crave, so mote it be.

The Go, Head Lice Spell

One common problem in school-age kids is head lice. There are lotions that you can buy at your local pharmacy to help, but here is also a potion from the past.

Put fifty milliliters of castor oil in a bottle. Put ten drops of tea tree essential oil, ten drops of lavender essential oil, five drops of peppermint oil, and five drops of bergamot oil into the castor oil and shake it all up. Name and date the potion. As you shake it up, say this spell:

Little mites, be gone.
Let this spell send you on the run.
Stay away from my little one.
So mote it be.

Massage the oil into dry hair and leave it on for a good hour, if you can. Make sure you massage the oil behind the ears and everywhere on the child's head. Start to comb out the lice with the oil still on. Then use cool water to wash everything away and an antiseptic shampoo in a final wash. Do this for seven nights, depending on the severity of the infestation.

If you have never used any of these oils on a child before, do a little skin test first. Dab a little of the mixture on the back, just below the neck, and wait for twenty-four hours to see if there is a reaction before applying it to the head. If the child is allergic to any of the essential oils, you can omit or change the quantities. Further, tea tree oil also works on its own. However, do not use it straight from the bottle and undiluted on the scalp of young children. Always mix it with a carrier oil. For example, mix about three drops of tea tree oil with about nine drops of carrier oil, such as almond, jojoba, or even olive oil.

A Happy Marriage Spell

There are many marriage spells, and there is even a recipe for a happy marriage cake. Write out ten points of what, in your view, a happy marriage needs; for example, equality,

respect, a sense of humor, and so on. Study them after you have written them down and roll the paper up in your hand like a scroll. Light a dark red candle and say these words:

> *Jupiter and Juno, blessed be.*
> *Help my marriage to be happy.*
> *Love and affection fill every room.*
> *Kind and loving we both shall be.*
> *Let our voices each be heard.*
> *Equal two, parts of the one.*
> *An' it harm none,*
> *so mote it be.*

Then, holding the scroll, carefully burn it and bury the remains in the garden.

Help Me Survive the Holidays Spell

Whether it is summer vacation or Christmas, during any holiday season, there will be days fraught with "I'm bored" and "It's not fair" heard throughout the house. Try to limit those days with this spell at the beginning of the holidays.

Anoint a silver candle with lavender and sage oils and a gold candle with bergamot and rosemary oils. Light the candles and say these words:

> Blessed be to candle light.
> Let my children not fight.
> The holidays are upon us.
> Let them be full of fun and creativity.
> My children will play good.
> They will be joyous and happy.
> No more, my miserable brood.
> Candle light, blessed be.
> An' it harm none, so mote it be.

Throughout the holidays, whenever you need to recharge, light the candles when the children have gone to bed and it is peaceful, and repeat the spell.

A Pregnancy Stone Spell

This is a spell for expectant mothers who are worried or anxious. One of the stones that is perfect for expectant mothers is

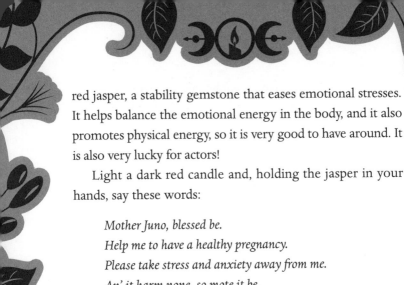

red jasper, a stability gemstone that eases emotional stresses. It helps balance the emotional energy in the body, and it also promotes physical energy, so it is very good to have around. It is also very lucky for actors!

Light a dark red candle and, holding the jasper in your hands, say these words:

Mother Juno, blessed be.
Help me to have a healthy pregnancy.
Please take stress and anxiety away from me.
An' it harm none, so mote it be.

Leave the stone near your bed at night and keep it with you throughout the day, carrying it in your purse.

Mother's Day Gratitude Spell

Our mothers gave us life; they nurtured us, and they worried for us. It is often said that mothers are angels in training. Yet how many times do we thank them? Although many of us have good relationships with our mothers, some people do not. If this is your situation, you may have a positive maternal figure in your life. And, there is also a mother who nurtures all of us: the Earth Mother. Goddess worship predates the patriarchal religions, so honoring our mother is nothing new.

Use this spell to create a talisman for your mother or maternal figure to show how grateful you are. Buy your mother a gift of jewelry, a bookmark, or something that she can wear or see every day. Hold it in your hand and say these words over it:

You kept me safe and loved.
And forever watch over me.
Thank you, mother, blessed be.

Every time your mother wears or looks at the object, she will know how grateful you are for her. If you do not have a mother for any reason, then equally show your gratitude to Mother Earth and bury a seed or plant in the ground to show your gratitude to the universe.

Father's Day Gratitude Spell

Father relationships can be wonderful, or they can be tumultuous, and yet Father's Day gifts and cards that appear in shops are growing in number yearly. Instead, try this gratitude spell for your father so he can see your gratitude and love daily. Buy a plant—such as an ivy, a maranta, or a coffee plant—and, on a small piece of paper, write your name. Fold it up tiny and squeeze it into the soil out of view. As you do, say,

> *Here is my love, which daily grows.*
> *Father's Day gratitude forever shows.*

Give your dad his plant and let him know it represents your love that will grow forever.

HEARTH

The hearth is the center of the home and provides warmth, light, food, and protection. One of the ways we protect our home is to ensure it's clean from germs and bacteria. However, there are other forms of cleaning that involve the supernatural and spiritual realms of cleansing, which can be done with salt, fire, air, and water, depending on what it is that needs to be cleaned. For example, to cleanse the pans that burn and spoil food, hold the pan in your right hand and sprinkle some sea salt into the pan. Wipe it around with a clean cloth using your left hand. Say,

> *In my hands, I wipe away all negativity.*
> *Cleansed and cleaned with no more bad energy.*

The reason we use the right side is that the right represents things we want to bring to us; the left side represents things we want to push away from us. By clearing something with your left hand, you are pushing the negativity away from you.

Something Lost Spell

There are times when items go missing for no apparent reason. Keys or jewelry—even things that you may have just put down—simply disappear. It's so frustrating. It could be absent-mindedness, but others believe that it's the mischievous work

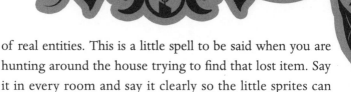

of real entities. This is a little spell to be said when you are hunting around the house trying to find that lost item. Say it in every room and say it clearly so the little sprites can hear you!

> Little sprites, I beseech thee,
> bring back my [lost item] to me.
> Little sprites, so mote it be.

Go about your daily chores or do something for ten minutes. Take your mind off your lost item and give the little sprites time to bring your item back. After, when you have recovered your lost items, remember to thank them.

The Happy Families Spell

Arrange a bouquet of angel's trumpet, hollyhock, peony, and iris. Place the flowers all around the house.

Anoint a gold candle with two drops of rosemary essential oil and two drops of lavender essential oil. Spray your holy water around the house to create a clear and harmonious atmosphere. After you have done this, light the candle and say these words:

Blessed be to my family,
forever strong and healthy.
Blessed be to be forever happy.
An' it harm none, so mote it be.

Afterward, open all the windows (no matter how cold) and let the air into every room. Breathe in the freshness and imagine the air bringing with it happy, positive energies.

Family Wishes Spell

Cut a heart shape out of some stiff cardboard and, as a family, gather things that you have collected on a family holiday or trip. This could be shells, small pebbles, flowers from a garden, or acorns and pinecones. If, however, you haven't been on a holiday or simply haven't collected anything, you can always use pictures or photos of your vacation.

Another good alternative is to create an imaginary vacation of the places you want to go with your family, thinking of all the things you want to see and do. You can even get creative with photoshop and create images of yourself standing in front of famous landmarks and use them to decorate your heart. Whatever you choose to use, perform the spell the same way.

Make a little hole at the top of the heart for a piece of ribbon to go through, as you are going to hang up your wishes so you can see them all year round. Then, as a family, on little heart pieces of cardstock, write wishes and hang them onto your main heart. Hang the heart up, and as you do so, say these words:

> *I wish I may, I wish I might,*
> *let my family have their wish this night.*
> *Blessed be to one and all. So mote it be.*

Throughout the year, when the family needs a little boost, touch the heart and remember your holiday and how happy you all were.

My Pet Spell

This is a spell to use when a beloved family pet has gone missing. Place some food in their bowl and light a green candle near their bowl. Recite this spell three times:

My pet has gone astray.
I wish for their return today.
Keep them from harm.
Return them to my arms.

Make posters including a recent photo of your pet and put them around the neighborhood for people to see. Your pet may have wandered off and gotten a bit lost.

Like You Spell

Friends are everything in this world. Many of us tell friends more secrets than we would tell our families. Perform this gratitude spell on a Sunday during a full moon.

Light a blue candle and give thanks for having such a good friend. Then say into the flame,

Like you, like me.
Friends together, forever be.
Like me, like you.
Friends forever true.

Put a photo up of you and your friend in a place where you will see it daily.

Family and Friends Protection Spell

Here is a specific spell for protection for your family or friends.

Write out the names of your family and friends and have the names in view as you light an orange candle. Then say these words:

> *Bless this family, bless this home.*
> *Wherever we may wander.*
> *Wherever we may roam.*
> *Let our love shine throughout our family.*
> *Let us be safe and protected wherever we may be.*
> *An' it harm none, so mote it be.*

Good Pals Charm

Good friends are hard to find, and friendships are harder to keep in this fast-moving world. For many of us, our friends are closer than our family, and they are the first people we talk to if we have a problem.

Try to find something in nature that comes in twos, such as shells or leaves or two acorns growing together (which are very rare). Have a photo of the two of you together and place the nature object on top of the photo. Then say over it,

Where you are, I can be.
Whenever you are in need.
Here I am, you will be.
Whenever I am in need.

Split the nature object. Keep a piece, and give the other piece to your friend. Tell them to keep it always with them, such as in their handbag or on a shelf—somewhere it will be seen every day.

The Phone Scrying Unwanted Houseguest Spell

If you feel as though there is something not right in your home, use your phone to verify this. In the past, a scrying bowl or spirit quartz would be used to see things. However, we have something just as good in our modern day and age, and that is the black screen of our phone, TV, laptop, and so on. These

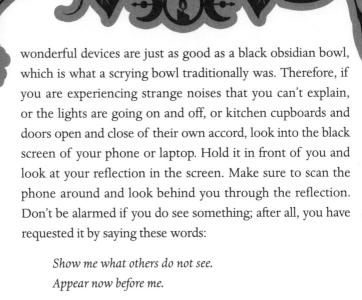

wonderful devices are just as good as a black obsidian bowl, which is what a scrying bowl traditionally was. Therefore, if you are experiencing strange noises that you can't explain, or the lights are going on and off, or kitchen cupboards and doors open and close of their own accord, look into the black screen of your phone or laptop. Hold it in front of you and look at your reflection in the screen. Make sure to scan the phone around and look behind you through the reflection. Don't be alarmed if you do see something; after all, you have requested it by saying these words:

> *Show me what others do not see.*
> *Appear now before me.*

If there is a presence in the house and it is becoming a nuisance, ask it to leave. You can always contact your local spiritualist church or a medium for help, and there are many people online who can advise you on dealing with unwanted guests—especially the ones that go bump in the night!

The subject of the family has many areas of concern that all flow from one another. Protection is a key part of the hearth and home, as we all want our family and loved ones to be safe. It is even more important now with the use of smart technology that is coming into our daily living. Magic and spells will need to change to accommodate these new ways, because, even though we are technologically advanced, we can still be affected with the same problems that our ancestors experienced, from challenging family relationships, to unwanted guests, to all the stresses and woes that are experienced on a daily basis.

MORE HOME AND HEARTH CORRESPONDENCES

Here is a list of additional resources you can use as substitutions in the family spells. You can also use these correspondences to create your own spells to fit your own situation, as all the resources listed here have their harmonics in tune with the subject of family.

Herbs

Acorns can be used for protection, strength, success, stability, healing, and fertility.

Bay laurel (and also *garlic*) is good for protection and good luck.

Carrot seed helps with fertility.

Sage can clear the atmosphere in the home of any evil feeling. Other methods are the ringing of a bell and using magic salt and holy water.

Vervain is a powerful all-purpose herb.

Crystals

Falcon's eye for boosting sexuality and encouraging pregnancy (and for sunburns!).

Jade for fertility and for challenging situations and protection; it was once known as "the warrior's stone."

Orange calcite for sexuality and confidence; it is also a good stone for students studying science.

Red jasper for convalescence and pregnancy.

Sardonyx for strength, protection, and a happy marriage.

Essential Oils

Cinnamon oil is antibacterial and antifungal; it also helps deaden the nerve where there is a toothache.

Lettuce oil promotes male fertility. Lettuce was sacred to Min, the Egyptian god of fertility.

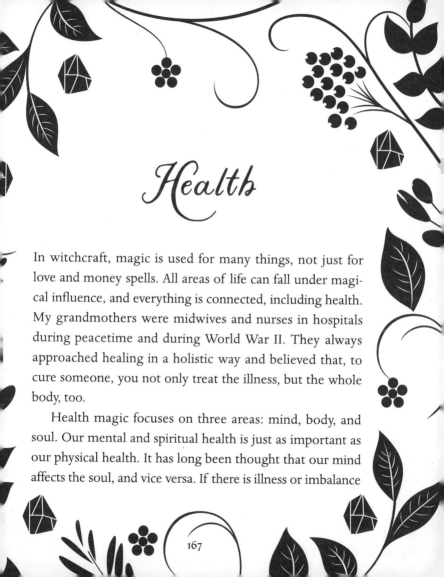

Health

In witchcraft, magic is used for many things, not just for love and money spells. All areas of life can fall under magical influence, and everything is connected, including health. My grandmothers were midwives and nurses in hospitals during peacetime and during World War II. They always approached healing in a holistic way and believed that, to cure someone, you not only treat the illness, but the whole body, too.

Health magic focuses on three areas: mind, body, and soul. Our mental and spiritual health is just as important as our physical health. It has long been thought that our mind affects the soul, and vice versa. If there is illness or imbalance

in one area, all areas will be affected. The term we use for this is *psyche and soma*, or *mind and body*.

The gods and goddesses who can be called upon in health matters are Apollo and his son Asclepius, Artemis, Brigid, and Eir, a Norse goddess who is the designated spirit of medicine and women's health. Febris was the Roman goddess of fever, so she is useful to know, and we can also call upon Raphael, who is the angel of healing.

Some herbs are just a bit better than others in creating that healthy feeling we long for. Fresh herbs are always best, and just a handful will do. Wash them and pop them into a teapot, pour boiling water over them, and let them brew for five to twenty minutes, then strain them and pour the tea into a cup. Sit back and enjoy your healthy infused tea.

Here are four of the best herbs for healing work:

FENNEL

Fennel is rich in oils that ease bloating, gas pains, and digestive spasms in both the small and large intestines. Fennel can also reduce bad breath and body odor that originates in the intestines. Hedgewitches have often used fennel for women

who are breastfeeding as it increases milk flow. We call this herb "the maiden's herb" because of its uses to enhance breasts and regulate hormones.

OREGANO

A sometimes-overlooked herb, but a powerhouse plant that contains at least four compounds that soothe coughs and nineteen chemicals with antibacterial properties that help reduce body odor. Oregano also helps with the digestive tract and can lower blood pressure.

ROSEMARY

Rosemary contains almost twenty chemicals with antibacterial properties that help fight infection. Rosemary has also been shown to prevent cataracts. Hedgewitches have traditionally used it to treat asthma and other allergies. We have also used rosemary to ease breast pain as it acts as a drying agent to fluid-filled cysts. We call this herb "the mother's herb."

SAGE

The sacred herb used for everything magical, medicinal, and culinary. Great for protection and consecration while also being the ultimate antiseptic and antibiotic. Hence, sage is the go-to herb for fighting bacteria and infections. It is also used to ease the symptoms of menopause, such as night sweats and hot flashes. Further, sage can be used for diabetes, as studies have shown that sage boosts insulin's action. We view sage as "the crone's or elder's herb."

Before we continue, just a word of warning: the remedies and spells here are only a guide. Always consult a medical practitioner or pharmacist if symptoms persist. Moreover, if you are already consulting a doctor, tell them that you intend to use herbal remedies and check whether these are fine alongside your conventional medication. Always listen to your doctor and never change your prescription unless told to by medical professionals.

QUICK REFERENCE
CORRESPONDENCE CHART

Colors	blue and white
Crystals	amethyst
Flower	jasmine
Incense	mint
Oil	basil
Day	Monday and Thursday
Deities	Asclepius
Planet	Jupiter
Numbers	1 and 7

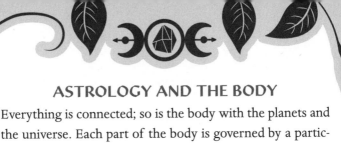

ASTROLOGY AND THE BODY

Everything is connected; so is the body with the planets and the universe. Each part of the body is governed by a particular planet. I have been taught to heal in accordance with this chart and its correspondence. At the end of this chapter, there is another chart that details the herbs and plants to use when treating these areas in relation to the correspondence.

Each zodiac sign rules a certain part of the body:

Aries: the head and brain

Taurus: the throat

Gemini: the lungs and nervous system

Cancer: the stomach and breasts

Leo: the heart area

Virgo: the abdomen

Libra: the kidneys and lower back

Scorpio: the sex organs

Sagittarius: the hips and thighs

Capricorn: the skeleton, teeth, and skin

Aquarius: the circulatory system

Pisces: the feet and the lymphatic system

However, this does not necessarily mean that the specified parts are "susceptible" to those zodiac signs or that they are weak spots. Indeed, it can mean that these are key areas that have extra strength; for example, Pisceans are the natural-born dancers of the zodiac, but they also need to develop preventative measures, such as always making sure shoes fit well. Also, Pisces rules the lymphatic system, which flushes out toxins, so making sure to drink enough water helps with this.

BODY

Physical Health

The body is a highly complex system, and it changes throughout our lives. We need to keep our bodies in optimum health through exercise and eating the right nutrients to fight viruses and illnesses that may develop. Some people are very lucky and never seem to develop anything, but one thing is for sure, and that is that no one can stop the effects of time on our bodies, as this is the natural progression of

change as we venture into old age. These spells are specifically for the changes and ailments in the body that most of us experience at some point in our lives.

The Menopause Spell

When it comes to menopause, everyone is different. Some sail through the experience without a thought, while others struggle. Pomegranates and cranberries are helpful during menopause as they are packed with important nutrients, such as vitamin C and antioxidants. Make a pomegranate and cranberry punch and drink it throughout the day to help lower blood pressure and cholesterol.

Here is a spell especially written for those who are suffering with this natural aspect of aging. Light one red candle and one blue candle and say these words:

> *Body changes throughout time.*
> *The maid and the mother have been mine.*
> *In one form or another.*
> *Changes now to the next phase have I.*
> *Hot flashes, a constant fight.*

I embrace the body, mind, and soul.
Body changes throughout time.
I embrace these changes of mine.

The Magic Gargle Spell

Agate is a good stone to use for sore throats, so we are going to make a gargle mixture with it. Take a piece of agate and drop it into some drinking water. Over the water, say or whisper,

Blessed agate, heal me, please.
My throat is sore and full of pain.
Let me not have this again.
Blessed agate, take away my sore throat.
Blessed be. So mote it be.

Take out the stone, put a teaspoonful of your magic sea salt into the water, and mix it in. Gargle with the water as often as you can. You could also make agate water. Drop the agate in drinking water and leave it for about ten minutes, then take it out. You can sip the water all day. Always make

sure that your agate is clean before you begin making any elixirs.

An Arthritis Pain Spell

There are a few crystals that can help with arthritis: green aventurine, apatite, and chrysoprase. See if you can find a piece of jewelry, such as a bracelet, made out of chrysoprase. Light a purple candle and hold the crystal in your hands as you petition the angel Raphael. Archangel Raphael is the angel of healing and is good to call upon when pain relief and healing are needed:

> *Blessed Raphael, hear me, please,*
> *heal my pain with your touch.*
> *Angel Raphael, thank you. Blessed be.*

Keep holding the stone and place it on the part that hurts. If you have a piece of chrysoprase jewelry, keep wearing it. Every so often, recharge the crystal or jewelry with this ritual.

Period Pain Spell

Lavender oil is good for period pain when massaged into the stomach. Aquamarine can also help with hormonal problems and period pain. Make yourself some rosemary tea: boil the water and pour it over a couple of fresh sprigs of rosemary, leave it for five minutes, and then sweeten it with honey. Rosemary is a very versatile herb and can regulate the menstrual cycle. Liquorice tea can also improve digestion and soothe menstrual pain.

Rub some liquorice oil into an aquamarine stone. Hold it over your body where you have the pain and say this spell:

> *Mother goddess, such pain have I.*
> *From month to month, suffer do I.*
> *Help me please, from month to month.*
> *An' it harm none, so mote it be.*

Keep the aquamarine as close to your body throughout the day as you can, perhaps keeping it in a skirt or trouser pocket—wherever the pain hurts the most.

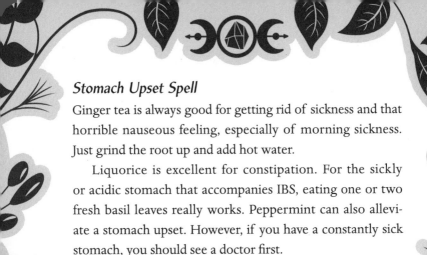

Stomach Upset Spell

Ginger tea is always good for getting rid of sickness and that horrible nauseous feeling, especially of morning sickness. Just grind the root up and add hot water.

Liquorice is excellent for constipation. For the sickly or acidic stomach that accompanies IBS, eating one or two fresh basil leaves really works. Peppermint can also alleviate a stomach upset. However, if you have a constantly sick stomach, you should see a doctor first.

The stone beryl can help heal and regulate the stomach. Infuse a piece of beryl or beryl jewelry with some ginger oil. While rubbing the ginger oil into the beryl, say these words:

> Stomach upsets, be gone.
> Sickness and heartburn, be free.
> An' it harm none, so mote it be.

Hold the stone over your stomach or wear the beryl jewelry every day.

Headache Spell

A headache can indicate serious underlying problems, so please seek medical attention if you are suffering from chronic headaches.

At the same time, there are some herbal remedies you could use instead of reaching for the pills. Lemons are renowned for their healing properties. The first thing to try is a cup of bergamot (Earl Grey) tea with a slice of lemon in it. Or, you could cut the rind off a lemon, mash it into a paste, and apply it to your forehead; have some prepped and in the fridge so that it's cool when you need it. If the pain is too great to be messing around with making a paste, cut two slices of lemon and apply them to the temples while saying these words:

> *Gods, hear me please,*
> *let my pain ease.*
> *Take away the pain in my head.*
> *I do not want to spend the day in bed.*
> *Blessed gods, hear me please.*
> *An' it harm none, so mote it be.*

If you can, lie down for a while with the lemon slices on your forehead. If you have repeated headaches, see a doctor.

Fever Spell

Fevers often accompany a virus, and the fever is the first indication that something is wrong. When a fever comes on, first seek professional medical advice.

There are a few things you can do with fevers alongside medical regiments: keep hydrated by drinking water, wear very light clothing, and keep the air circulating. As always, rest is best.

Febris is the Roman goddess of fevers, and she was often called upon to ease a fever. Try this spell:

> *Goddess Febris, blessed be,*
> *please take care of me.*
> *This fever will break, and I will be well.*
> *Goddess Febris, please hear my spell.*
> *So mote it be.*

If the fever persists, call a doctor, and if it rises, seek medical attention immediately.

A Toothache Spell

Try this spell if you are suffering from a toothache and cannot get to the dentist immediately. However, even after the pain goes away, go see the dentist to identify the underlying problems and cause of the toothache.

A piece of amber, jet, or malachite is good for tooth pain; rub some clove oil onto any of these stones. As you do so, say these words:

> *Toothache, be gone.*
> *An' it harm none,*
> *So mote it be.*

Hold the stone over the side of your mouth where the pain is. You could also sleep with the stone under your pillow.

A Bad Back Massage Oil

Mix fifty milliliters of a carrier oil, such as sweet almond, with four drops each of chamomile, rosemary, ginger, and lavender essential oils. Put a couple of drops of lavender and eucalyptus oils into bathwater and relax in the water before drying off and applying the massage oil. Afterward, rest and

meditate upon your back. Imagine a lavender color, warming and healing, swirling into your back and taking the pain away.

For a Friend in Need

Anoint a blue candle with lavender, cedar, and geranium oils. When the candle is ready, push a needle halfway into it (you can choose where on the candle you want to stick the needle). Whatever the complaint of your friend is, write it down and sprinkle some lavender over the words. Then light the candle and say,

> My friend [name] is in need.
> Please, universe, his/her/their illness ease,
> let his/her/their pain be gone.
> An' it harm none.
> Universe, blessed be.
> So mote it be.

You can repeat this spell each night while your friend is suffering. Each time the candle burns down to the needle,

extinguish it, and move the needle farther down when the candle is cold.

Acne Spell

First, make a skin wash with two drops of calendula flower oil and a thyme water rinse. Check your proprietary facial wash to see if it already has calendula in it—you may be surprised. To make the thyme water, boil some water and pour it over some fresh thyme; then bottle it and keep it for rinsing.

Now, take an egg and clean it by making a hole at the top and bottom of the egg and blowing the insides out. Wash the egg out and leave it to dry. Sprinkle some thyme, lavender, and dandelion into the egg, and say these words:

> *Universe, set me free.*
> *Take away this acne.*
> *The egg that breaks,*
> *my acne will take.*
> *An' it harm none,*
> *So mote it be.*

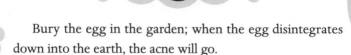

Bury the egg in the garden; when the egg disintegrates down into the earth, the acne will go.

There are also teas you can use, such as dandelion and burdock, to help the body release toxins, skin bacteria, and excess hormones, all of which cause acne.

Vomiting (Magic Stomach Powder)

Ginger is always best for stomach upsets. However, there is an old Eastern remedy that, apparently, was even known in King Solomon's time. It calls for cinnamon and cardamom.

Grind three cinnamon sticks and one teaspoon of cardamom together with a pestle and mortar to create a powder. Keep this powder in a special bottle, labeled and dated. Pour boiling water over a teaspoonful of the stomach powder and sip it slowly to bring relief.

Sore Feet Soak

In a bowl of water, put a tablespoonful of your magic sea salt and two drops each of lavender and rose essential oils. Leave the feet to soak.

Magic Sunburn Lotion Spell

Always be sensible in the sun and apply sunscreen. However, if you have a mild case of sunburn, here are a couple of remedies. One is natural yogurt, which can be used as a cream. You can also apply a compress of vinegar and cucumber juice or even cold tea.

For a special lotion, put four teaspoons of lemon juice, eight teaspoons of sweet almond oil, two teaspoons of honey (preferably clear), and one teaspoon of water in a screw top jar and shake it well. As you do so, say these words:

> *Dear Apollo, god of the sun,*
> *forgive me, for I have been too long,*
> *in your watchful gaze.*
> *I long to be outside for days and days.*
> *Forgive me, Apollo, and help me please.*
> *Send me sunburn ease.*
> *An' it harm none, so mote it be.*

Apply the lotion thoroughly and, if you can stand it, massage the oil into your skin.

MIND

Mental Health

The mind for many is still a mystery. There is still so much doctors do not know; every year, neurologists and psychiatrists are making new discoveries. The mind and the diseases of the mind destroy many lives each year. Stress and physical conditions of the brain create pain and anxiety in both the patient and their loved ones. It is important to address the mind when healing in a holistic manner. The next couple of spells are all about the mind and trying rebalance the psyche and soma effects.

Psyche and Soma Detox Spell

To rebalance the mind, body, and soul, start to integrate a detox regime in your lifestyle. One of the easiest ways to detox is to make healthy smoothies. Start your detox regime off by making a healthy smoothie with plenty of fruit and vegetables. Try an antioxidant boost drink by blending apples and red berries, such as raspberries and strawberries, together with some lemon and ginger.

Put all ingredients in a blender and conjure up some universal detox by saying,

> Hubble, bubble, I've toiled and I'm troubled.
> Here in this drink, a mind, body, and soul mix.
> The stress and woe I need to nix.

Enjoy your drink and remember to drink plenty of water throughout your day.

Child Illness Spell

Illnesses can be very frightening for young children who have not experienced illness before, so this is a little spell for children who may be frightened:

> Goddess Brigid, I beseech,
> let my child be well.
> Heal their wounds and dry their tears.
> Let them fight this illness with your strength.
> Goddess Brigid, hear my spell.
> Gracious Brigid, blessed be.
> An' it harm none, so mote it be.

Evening Primrose Happy Memories Spell

If you have had a particularly happy day and want to make sure you always remember these sweet memories, cast this spell in the evening as the evening primrose is coming out.

Light a yellow candle, retrieve a notebook or diary, and write about the day. After you have recorded what happened, say this spell over the words with your evening primrose nearby.

> *Remember always the memories of today.*
> *Sweet and gentle, warm and true.*
> *Remember them when pain comes my way.*
> *Delicious memories I have of you.*

Read what you have written and meditate on how wonderful the day has been.

Heal My Heart of Grief Spell

Grief is a condition that affects people in many ways. There is the emotional pain, but there's also a physical aspect to it. After a loved one has passed the traditional mourning period used to be a year, but in our modern times, we are lucky to be allowed a few days off work. However, life goes back to normal—or does it? In a period of grieving, we ourselves can suffer from numerous ailments that previously we would have recovered from easily. But now it may take weeks, so we need to heal the body, too.

Make a white candle with lily oil during a full moon. Light the candle and say these words:

> *Gracious mother, heal my heart.*
> *A loved one has passed.*
> *Heart, body, and mind,*
> *need strength, love in kind.*
> *Gracious mother, hear my spell,*
> *make my body well.*
> *Gracious mother, blessed be.*
> *An' it harm none, so mote it be.*

Meditate on the candle and let its warmth penetrate into your heart. Leave the candle to burn safely for as long as possible before blowing it out.

A Depression Spell

Depression is a serious illness and, like any other, needs to be treated by a medical professional. Contact your doctor if you are suffering with bouts of depression. Follow your instincts. If you are tired, then sleep. Relax, meditate, and pamper yourself. Look after yourself. Treat yourself like a god or goddess; you are divine and unique, after all.

Alongside needed professional medical care, pamper yourself with a relaxing herbal soak. Put two drops each of lavender, juniper, rose, clove, and bay essential oils into your bathwater. Soak in the water and relax. Imagine a white healing light emanating from the water. When you get out of the bath, imagine that feeling of the water still comforting you and say,

> *Sacred waters, send me release,*
> *from this sadness and depression.*
> *Sacred waters, let my illness heal.*
> *Sacred waters, blessed be. So mote it be.*

When you feel the depression sweeping over you again, remember the warm comforting bath and say the spell again, but also contact your doctor.

A Sleep Spell

In our very busy world, it can be difficult to switch off. There are a few things that can help. Howlite is a good relaxation crystal, the herb jasmine encourages sweet dreams, and passionflower brings a deep peaceful sleep. Hold a piece of howlite and rub two drops of jasmine essential oil onto it as you say,

> *Sleep, sleep, sleep, come to me.*
> *Sleep, sleep, sleep. So mote it be.*

Keep the jasmine under your pillow and allow yourself to drift off. Peppermint tea can also aid insomnia.

SOUL

Spiritual Health

There is a term that has been around now for a couple of decades, and that is *work-life balance*—but how many of

us can truly say we have that balance? Our working lives can seriously contribute to our physiological health. The ancients called it "psyche and soma"—literally, "mind and body."

Modern medical researchers have discovered that there is a two-way communication happening between the brain and the body. These little messenger chemicals link the brain to the body, and vice versa. Indeed, our thoughts create a physical response in our bodies. For example, by simply altering your breathing, you can change the feeling of pain.

We must take care of every aspect within this divine trinity, and this begins with our physical lives and finding a work-life balance.

For example, if we are happy with our jobs, then we are healthy in ourselves. If we are unhappy at work, we take time off. Then we feel guilty for having time off, which further adds to our poor health. How many people get ill at the onset of a holiday? Our bodies are finally allowed to relax, and suddenly we feel tired, drained, and ill. If our working lives do not change, there is a possibility that autoimmune diseases will become the next plague of generations, young and old.

We need to find balance between our work and our lives before it is too late. The psyche and soma debate rages on, and although we seek to unite the mind and body with a healthy diet and lifestyle, we must remember the other aspect of psyche, and that is the soul. If we are to be truly healthy, we must have a positive spiritual life. Our lives must be completely balanced. When we have faith, we are strong, for we feel and know we are not alone. The work that the spiritual community does is paramount to the overall health of all. The quest for a work-life balance needs to also address the soul. Only then can we truly be complete.

Work-Life Balance Spell

We need to reconnect with the earth and rebalance ourselves, and the best way to do this is to be out in nature or to invite nature into the home by buying a plant. We need to feel connected once more. Buy a positive plant that is good for harmonizing the environment, such as aloe vera or

English ivy. As you place it in your home somewhere you will see it every day, say these words:

> I work both day and night.
> On life's work, I toil.
> But rebalance is needed to put right,
> to stop me my soul's boil.
> No more live to work,
> but work to live and enjoy the earth's soil.

Then, lighting a white candle, say these words:

> Open my eyes so that I can see.
> The signs that are happening to me.
> I will not fear, and I will not recoil.
> The changes surrounding me.
> I am listening, I will not flinch.
> Whispered voices carried on a breeze.
> Universe of wonder, blessed be.

Be still and meditate on the flame. You may begin to see images forming or to feel inspired; this is called "clairsen-

tience," which is an all-feeling, all-knowing gift from the universe to help you.

Be Happy Charm

Cut a circle the size of a small bottle lid out of bright yellow cardstock. Make a smiley face on it, then hold it in your hand as you say,

> *Sunshine yellow, happy face.*
> *Bring light and laughter to every place.*
> *Be happy, happy forever be.*
> *An' it harm none, so mote it be.*

Place your smiley face in your purse or wallet and take it with you wherever you go. When you feel unhappy, take out your charm, hold it in your hands, close your eyes, and remember your happy memories.

Playtime Spell

We are so wrapped up in duty and responsibility that we can lose ourselves and our sense of fun. In order to enjoy life in a healthy manner, we need to reconnect with the child within

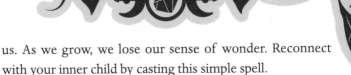

us. As we grow, we lose our sense of wonder. Reconnect with your inner child by casting this simple spell.

Find a picture of you when you were about five or six years old. Light an orange candle, sprinkle some multicolored glitter on your photo, and say,

> *I am grown but need to seek,*
> *the child hidden within me.*
> *Innocence, return to me.*
> *Wonder in all I see.*

Blow out the candle and watch the majesty of the smoke rising with your spell upon its dancing circles. After, go for a walk in nature, such as a park, and embrace all the wonder of nature.

RESTORATION RETREAT

It is easy to say our lifestyles are slowly killing us, but if we delve deeper into this statement, we can see how truly out of balance we really are. We need to find the harmony once more between the mind, body, and soul. Therefore, try to create a restoration and rejuvenation retreat at least once a month. Try one weekend out of three; give yourself a treat.

Friday Night Ritual: Zodiac Healing Tea

In magic, everything is connected. Every correspondence influences something else. It is important to drink the right tea to create inner balance. The universe plays a huge part in what kind of tea, plant, or flower is good for you depending on your sun sign.

Start your magical restoration weekend by brewing up some herbal tea instead of reaching for the wine. Traditionally, tea is made from the leaves of the tea plant and is believed to have originated in China. However, teas made with herbs are just as valuable for medicinal purposes, sweetened with our favorite spices or honey. It is a well-known fact that an infusion of ginger, hot water, and lemon is ideal for coughs and colds. And we are finding out now that green tea may help reduce the risk of heart disease and some forms of cancer. Tea in general contains L-theanine, which is associated with producing a calm but alert mental state by affecting the brain's alpha waves, which is probably why so many

of us have tea as our first drink of the day. Wake up to tea and a good morning!

However, if you would like to create your own tea for a personal boost, especially one corresponding to your sun sign, below are some potential flavors you could use. You can buy loose green or black tea leaves and add the dried fruits and flowers pertaining to your sun sign to produce the tea you desire. If you do not like your assumed sun sign's taste, this might indicate which planets are more prevalent in your birth chart.

Light a gold candle, pour the tea, and say this spell as you slowly sip your tea:

> *Universe of light,*
> *planets of my birth,*
> *give me strength to fight.*
> *The days are long and hard.*
> *Replenish my strength with this tea.*
> *An' it harm none, so mote it be.*

Sun Sign Correspondences

Aries

Planet: Mars

Herbs: honeysuckle, cowslip, rosemary

Flowers and plants: poppy, holly, geranium, thistle

Vegetable: onion

Fruits: orange, pineapple

Taurus

Planet: Venus

Herbs: elder, lovage, spearmint

Flowers and plants: violet, rose, daisy, lily

Vegetable: potato

Fruits: apple, apricot

Gemini

Planet: Mercury

Herbs: lavender, hare's foot, fern

Flowers and plants: woodbine, lavender, lily of the valley

Vegetable: carrot
Fruits: raspberry, fig, date, passion fruit

Cancer
Planet: Moon
Herbs: saxifrage, hyssop, balm
Flowers and plants: water lily, wild flowers, marigold,
   willow
Vegetable: lettuce
Fruits: pear, pineapple

Leo
Planet: sun
Herbs: bay, borage, angelica, cinnamon
Flowers and plants: daffodil, sunflower, chamomile, citrus
   trees
Vegetable: pumpkin
Fruits: orange, lemon

Virgo

Planet: Mercury

Herbs: caraway, myrtle, fennel

Flowers and plants: small flowers, fennel, barley wheat

Vegetable: carrot

Fruits: raspberry, plum

Libra

Planet: Venus

Herbs: daisy, garden mint

Flowers and plants: pansy, orchid, white rose, vine

Vegetable: potato

Fruits: apple, peach

Scorpio

Planets: Pluto, Mars

Herbs: broom, hops, basil

Flowers and plants: heather, blackthorn, rhododendron

Vegetables: Jerusalem artichoke, onion
Fruits: pomegranate, pineapple, dark red grape

Sagittarius

Planet: Jupiter
Herbs: moss, sage, dandelion
Flowers and plants: lime, oak, mulberry, pink flowers
Vegetable: asparagus
Fruits: blueberry, banana

Capricorn

Planet: Saturn
Herbs: comfrey, hemlock, beet
Flowers and plants: pine, ivy, carnation, black poppy
Vegetable: beetroot
Fruits: coconut, pear

Aquarius

Planets: Saturn, Uranus
Herbs: sorrel, quince, heart's ease

Flowers and plants: myrrh, orchid, most fruit trees, frankincense

Vegetables: beansprout, beetroot

Fruits: strawberry, coconut, rhubarb

Pisces

Planets: Jupiter, Neptune

Herbs: dock, sage, fig

Flowers and plants: water lily, willow tree, moss, fern

Vegetables: asparagus, mushroom

Fruits: blueberry, melon, cherry, almond

Relaxing Sunday Bath: Healing Bath Spell

Soak up the magical healing power of water and salts with this easy homemade bath recipe.

In a bowl, mix two hundred grams (eight ounces) each of sea salt and Epsom salts. Slowly add one or two drops of your chosen essential oil along with herbs and flowers, if you wish. Grind the flowers and herbs in a blender before adding them to the salt, but you could always keep them as natural

as possible. Store your bath salts in a sealed container and sprinkle a few tablespoons into a warm bath. Allow them to dissolve before soaking and purifying yourself. Epsom salts are great for this, but any salt is good. Try the Himalayan pink salt for an extra boost.

Belisama is the Celtic goddess of water, and as you relax in the bath, allowing the healing salts to soothe your body, cast a spell asking for the powers of healing within the water.

> *Lady of water, lady of healing.*
> *Weary and tired I am feeling.*
> *Renew my strength and power.*
> *Fighting fit in every hour.*

This section on healing has discussed the complex systems within our bodies and our world. We have looked at certain conditions, but realize there are countless other spells for various ailments. However, in all that you do, you should always trust your instincts—pain is always a warning—and consult a doctor if something is wrong. Have a checkup

every so often. The times we live in are indeed very stressful, so try to find time for yourself. If in doubt, make that appointment.

MORE HEALTH CORRESPONDENCES

Here is a list of additional resources you can use as substitutions in the health spells. You can also use these correspondences to create your own health spells to fit your own situation, as all the resources listed here have their harmonics in tune with the subject of health and mind, body and soul.

Herbs

Chamomile is also good for relaxing the nervous system.

Eucalyptus can rejuvenate the body and spirit.

Raspberry leaf can be combined in equal parts with cut ginger root to make a tea; having steeped, this can be sipped slowly to end a fit of sneezing.

Crystals

Amber is good for the solar plexus, therefore healing the immune system, digestion, asthma, depression, and influenza.

Bloodstone can boost the immune system and aid self-protection.

Howlite is a calming stone often used to help insomnia.

Lepidolite is also said to aid sleep—pop a piece under your pillow.

Merlinite is an ideal stone for healing and for meditation.

Essential Oils

Aloe vera, *ginseng*, *horsetail*, and *myrrh* are all excellent healing oils.

Patchouli oil is used for balance and confidence.

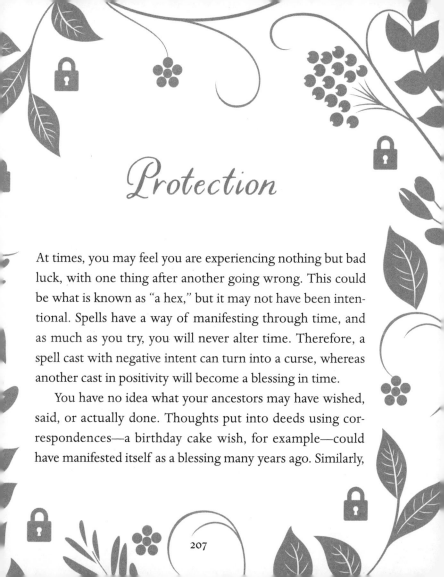

Protection

At times, you may feel you are experiencing nothing but bad luck, with one thing after another going wrong. This could be what is known as "a hex," but it may not have been intentional. Spells have a way of manifesting through time, and as much as you try, you will never alter time. Therefore, a spell cast with negative intent can turn into a curse, whereas another cast in positivity will become a blessing in time.

You have no idea what your ancestors may have wished, said, or actually done. Thoughts put into deeds using correspondences—a birthday cake wish, for example—could have manifested itself as a blessing many years ago. Similarly,

QUICK REFERENCE
CORRESPONDENCE CHART

Colors	black and white
Crystals	jet and spirit quartz
Flower	snapdragon or antirrhinum
Incense	dragon's blood
Oil	spikenard
Day	Saturday
Deities	Pluto
Planet	Saturn
Numbers	7 and 9

words spoken in anger to someone and an active deed of revenge may have manifested as a curse upon a family or a particular member of that family.

A hex usually lasts for a set time, anywhere from an hour to a year, while a curse can last a lifetime and can also follow through the bloodline of a family.

The ethics of spell weaving are very important—that is why you never interfere in the free will of someone. You never try to change someone into something they are not. We all have our own paths to follow and our own opinions; do not try to manipulate someone into your way of thinking by using magic, as it is likely to backfire on you. And, you could end up cursing yourself.

SPELLS

The Break a Spell

Sometimes it feels as if we are cursed—that someone has put a spell on us. You will need a black candle and your magic mirror to break this. The spell is to be done in a protected circle of salt. Light the candle and look into the mirror, saying these words:

I send this magic back,
through the candle black.
Go now from this place.
Never return to this face.
Mirror blessed, I beseech,
cloak of mirrors, cover me.
An' it harm none, so mote it be.

Keep staring into the mirror and imagine the curse or spell being lifted from you. Extinguish the flame, but not by blowing it out. Wrap the mirror up. Remember to keep it especially for magical work.

Wicked Spell

Use this spell to break a hex if you feel you have been cursed and nothing seems to be going right. However, please bear in mind that, as hard as it is to hear this, our lives wax and wane just like the moon and in nature. There is summer, but there is always winter. We have good times, and, unfortunately, we also have bad times. That is the way of the earth.

If you truly feel you have been cursed, try this spell. Light one black and one white candle, and while watching the flames of both, say these words:

Hear me, Mars, hear my plea.
Someone has cursed me.
Return their wicked thoughts threefold.
Justice Mars, like in times of old.

Keep the candles burning for about an hour and then snuff them out.

Bad Luck Chaser

This spell chases the bad luck away with a good luck invocation. Draw a large pentagram and write your full name in the center. Sprinkle a little sugar on the name. Drip some water onto it, and tear up some mint and clover leaves. Sprinkle the leaves onto the water, sugar, and name. As you do, say,

Good luck, come.
Come to stay.

Chase all the bad away.
Come at no delay.
This is my will, be done.
An' it harm none, so mote it be.

Stop Bad Luck Charm Bag

If you feel like you need an extra boost with eliminating negative experiences or you simply feel you've had a run of bad luck, create this charm bag and hang it up in your home, office, car, or all three, if you feel as though you need it.

Small green material bag

Angelica root

Ginger

Fennel seed

Holy thistle

Clove

Basil

Small citrine stone

During the full moon, put all ingredients together in the bag. Leave it in the light of the full moon to charge it.

As you do, say,

Blessed lady of the night.
Grant me luck that is right.

Make sure the bag is tied tightly and keep it with you whenever you feel bad luck is around.

Why Spell

Understanding human behavior can take a lifetime and be very painful to come to terms with. Some people can be really mean at times, so cast this spell if you simply have had enough of someone's negative behavior and if you find yourself constantly asking, "Why?"

Light a blue candle and sprinkle some salt on a flat surface. Then, with your index finger, draw their initial in the salt and say,

Why are you so mean?
Why can't life be like a dream?

Why do you have to make me scream?
Leave now and never return.
For you I will no longer yearn.

Columbine Protection Spell

In medieval times, every part of the plant was used in folk medicine. However, columbine is toxic and not suitable for self-medication. If you can, plant columbine around your house or grow some in a pot near the door. In the evening, cast this spell:

Mother goddess,
protect all therein,
evil shall not pass.
Columbine guardian.

Relationship Detox Spell

The pain we feel when we encounter toxic individuals who break our trust is excruciating. Yet we must learn from it and move on, no matter the difficulty. Look out for these individuals, and always be aware that toxic people do exist.

If you have any item given to you by the individual or a photograph of happier times with them, place it on top of your recipe book.

> We were friends, you and me,
> but you broke my trust and treat me cruelly.
> Be gone from my life for now and evermore.
> The likes of you stay away from my door.

Then, taking a pair of scissors, cut the photo and bury the pieces in the garden. If it is an item that they gave you, get rid of it. Say the words and waft incense over and all around it before giving it away.

The Backstabber Spell

This is probably one of the most painful toxic relationships you can come across in your working life. You could have worked with this person for years. You could have socialized with them. You could have even helped them out many times at work or have been a shoulder to cry on when things went wrong for them.

Yet the words *trust* and *betrayal* come to the fore with the backstabber. There is no easy way around this. However they have stuck the knife in deep, there is little you can do about it now. Perhaps they did what they did to save their own face and job. This is usually the case. The backstabber, at the end of the day, is a deeply selfish person, like all toxic people.

If possible, acquire a snapdragon flower or plant. If you cannot get one, a picture will suffice, but the real thing is best. As with herbs, dried flowers are fine, but the fresher, the better! You also need a mirror, a red pen or paper, and a tiger's eye crystal. This is a wonderful crystal and perfect for this occasion because it makes those who backstab you think twice; with the added kick of the mirror, we are going to send the betrayal right back to them.

In the light of an orange candle, place the snapdragon next to the tiger's eye. Write the culprit's name on a piece of paper; either the pen or the paper needs to be red. Stand the mirror behind the flame so that you can see your own face, as well as the snapdragon and tiger's eye, reflected in it. Say these words:

Your disloyal deeds I send back to thee.
Your thoughts and lies of deceit I return to thee.
[Name], no longer shall you give pain,
for I shall send it back to you again and again.
Snapdragon and tiger's eye will end your backstabbing ways.
Hours at work alone you shall be always.
No more shall I trust in thee.
For now, and evermore, so mote it be.

Keep the candle burning for as long as possible before extinguishing it properly. Keep the name, snapdragon, and mirror in view or on your altar for the next seven days. Take the tiger's eye with you to work and keep it with you at all times (or in your desk). After seven days, bury the snapdragon and paper in the garden, if possible. If you do not have a garden, burn the paper and dispose of everything in the usual mundane way.

The Bully Spell

There are so many bullies in the world nowadays that it is hard to describe what exactly they are like. Generally, when we think back to our experiences of school and remember the bully, they were probably physical and knocked us around a bit. The adult bully of the workforce could still do that, but they are likely to get sued.

Cast this spell on a Sunday evening while getting ready for the week ahead. Lighting an orange candle and visualizing the bully, stare into the flame and see the outcome you desire. When you are ready, say the spell:

> *You are weak and I am strong,*
> *I am right and you are wrong,*
> *you are a bully whom I will fight.*
> *And I will win for I am right.*

When you go to work in the morning, do not feel intimidated by the bully. Simply smile and gather as much proof as you can, then go to your union and the human resources department to state your case.

Talisman Activation Spell

A talisman can be absolutely anything you hold dear, from a necklace, to a ring, to even a handbag. Basically, anything can be a talisman if it is meaningful to you. When you first get your talisman, you need to cleanse and then charge it. You can cleanse it under running water, so hold it under the tap for a few minutes. Or, pass it through smoke from incense. Then leave it in the sun or moonlight to charge for a few hours. After holding it in your hands, concentrate upon it. Imagine all the things you want it to do and give you.

While still holding the talisman in your hands, say, "I dedicate this talisman of mine to the highest good of all who come in contact with it."

Use your talisman appropriately, either by wearing it or hanging it up in the home. It needs to be somewhere you can see it daily, and it needs to be out in the open, not locked away in a drawer or cupboard, as you want the light and the energy to swarm around it.

Here is a list of some lucky charms, talismans, and amulets people have used and still use to ward off evil and to stay clear of hexes and curses. How many do you have around your home?

Garlic

Copper bracelets

Egyptian scarabs

St. Christopher's medals

Four-leaf clovers

Letters of protection

Rings

Lucky coins

The cone from a hemlock tree

MORE PROTECTION CORRESPONDENCES

Here is a list of additional resources you can use as sub-stitutions in the protection spells. You can also use these correspondences to create your own spells to fit your own situation, as all the resources listed here have their harmon-ics in tune with the subject of protection and defense.

Herbs

Juniper is ideal for purification rituals, especially before com-mencing a banishing or cleansing spell.

Mugwort is traditionally used to cleanse energies and get rid of negativity.

White sage has been used for millennia by indigenous peoples around the world for purification and cleansing the atmosphere of homes, people who may be possessed, and items that may be cursed.

Palo santo is for the purification of the spirit and clearing negative energy in places and locations.

Crystals

Emerald is an ideal protection stone that dispels negativity in any relationship.

Fire agate is a perfect stone to counteract negative energies as it acts as a shield of protection around you.

Tiger's eye is the ultimate stone of protection for many people all over the world. Ideal for when you are in a negative relationship or working in a toxic office.

Black obsidian is an all-around brilliant stone that dispels negativity and gives the owner protection from all negative forces with evil intent.

Black tourmaline is another powerful stone that repels negative energies.

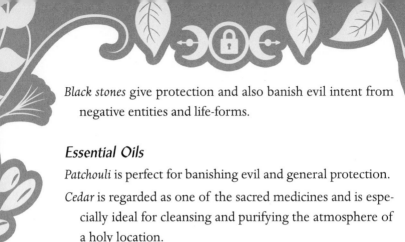

Black stones give protection and also banish evil intent from negative entities and life-forms.

Essential Oils

Patchouli is perfect for banishing evil and general protection.

Cedar is regarded as one of the sacred medicines and is especially ideal for cleansing and purifying the atmosphere of a holy location.

Myrrh is the holy oil used for sacred sanctification of items, people, and places.

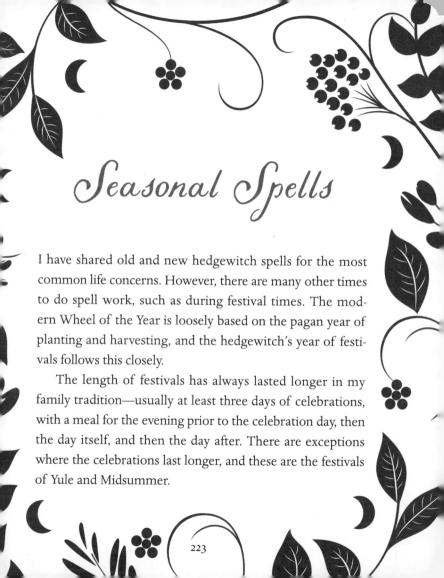

Seasonal Spells

I have shared old and new hedgewitch spells for the most common life concerns. However, there are many other times to do spell work, such as during festival times. The modern Wheel of the Year is loosely based on the pagan year of planting and harvesting, and the hedgewitch's year of festivals follows this closely.

The length of festivals has always lasted longer in my family tradition—usually at least three days of celebrations, with a meal for the evening prior to the celebration day, then the day itself, and then the day after. There are exceptions where the celebrations last longer, and these are the festivals of Yule and Midsummer.

Each festival has a set of elemental beings governing it. This chapter is dedicated to the festivals and accompanying spells to show how to harness the power of that festival.

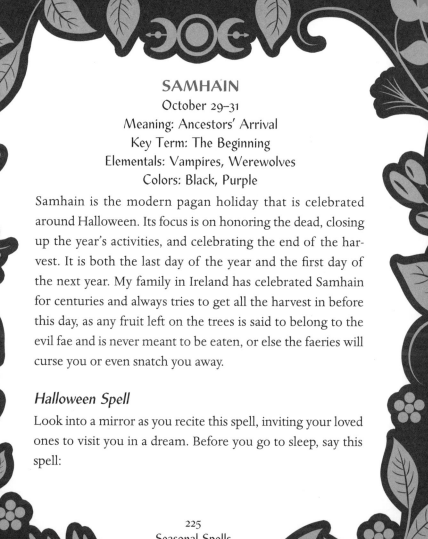

SAMHAIN
October 29–31
Meaning: Ancestors' Arrival
Key Term: The Beginning
Elementals: Vampires, Werewolves
Colors: Black, Purple

Samhain is the modern pagan holiday that is celebrated around Halloween. Its focus is on honoring the dead, closing up the year's activities, and celebrating the end of the harvest. It is both the last day of the year and the first day of the next year. My family in Ireland has celebrated Samhain for centuries and always tries to get all the harvest in before this day, as any fruit left on the trees is said to belong to the evil fae and is never meant to be eaten, or else the faeries will curse you or even snatch you away.

Halloween Spell

Look into a mirror as you recite this spell, inviting your loved ones to visit you in a dream. Before you go to sleep, say this spell:

Ancestors of my past,
please come to me at last.
Visit me in my dream this night.
But please do not give me a fright.
An' it harm none, so mote it be.

Go to sleep and try to remember the messages your departed loved ones gave you by writing them in your recipe book upon waking.

Angel's Trumpet Astral Traveling Spell

Given its powerful magical properties, the angel's trumpet is the perfect plant to use when astral projecting or journeying to other realms. Use an image of angel's trumpet if you do not have a real one, and meditate upon the image at night in your garden. Light one white candle, and stare into the flame as you say,

Lift the veil and let me see.
The world beyond this reality.
Then bring me back to this place.
Renewed within this time and space.

Let go of all worries and feel your body relax. Feel yourself begin to rise, and embrace the journey.

The Pumpkin Spell

Place a Halloween pumpkin in the center of your room with the candle or light flickering inside it. Cast this spell to allow positive energies to enter your living space.

> Scare away all on this dark night,
> all those who would do me harm and give a fright.
> No dark entities shall enter here.
> Allowed only, energies who bring love and pure light.

Leave a bowl of sweets and a small glass of beer for the positive energies as a mark of respect.

Samhain True Love Spell

Light an orange candle or, if possible, have a fire. With your recipe book on hand, stare into the flames after reciting this spell:

> Let me see in the flames,
> who it is and the names,

of the one I will marry,
Samhain fire, grant me clarity.

Stare into the flames to see initials forming of the one you are meant to marry. Write them down in your recipe book.

YULE
December 21–January 1
Meaning: Solstice Dark
Key Term: The Sleep
Elementals: Elves, Dryads
Colors: Green, Red, Gold

Yule, or Midwinter, is the celebration of the winter solstice, the shortest day of the year. After that point, the sun begins to return to us, and the days get longer again.

There are many customs and traditions my family has to celebrate Yule. Evergreens, such as holly, ivy, and conifers, are used to symbolize the eternity of life, and fires are lit in honor of the god Thor. A Yule log is kept burning throughout to symbolize warmth; we remember it now with a chocolate Swiss roll cake. Candles are lit and Yule cakes are eaten.

Floral wreaths are hung on doors and green decorations are used.

Yule Blessing

On the first night of Yule, light a green candle anointed with pine essential oil and say,

> *Season of winter, you bring many changes.*
> *Season of winter, blessed be.*
> *Please do not bring sickness to me.*
> *Season of winter, let me be well.*
> *Season of winter, hear my spell.*
> *Season of winter, gifted of Yule.*
> *Bring blessings to me.*
> *An' it harm none, so mote it be.*

Repeat this spell on the last night of Yule to bring about blessings for the rest of winter.

Yule Log Spell

Go for a brisk walk on a winter's day in a park, forest, or wood, and find a small log. Hold the log in your arms and infuse it with happiness the whole year, keeping it in a special place or in the garden. The following Yule, you can burn it or bury it in the ground.

> *Blessed log of Yule.*
> *Grant my family wishes this day.*
> *Grant these all year to come my way.*
> *Wealth, love, and plenty of health.*
> *Send your Yule blessing to me.*
> *An' it harm none, so mote it be.*

Give thanks for all the good things the log brought throughout the year before repeating the spell with a new log.

Yule Snow Wish Spell

Use the weather to create love spells. Snow is the most versatile of all gifts from the goddess because it is so pure; it is basically a blank canvas, and you can use it for absolutely everything. Make a wish upon the snow for whatever you want or desire. You need to be out in the snow when you say this spell.

> *Snow, snow, everywhere and everyway.*
> *Grant me a wish upon this day.*
> *[Say what it is you wish for.]*

You need to say your wish spell seven times to make it work.

Yule Tree Popcorn Money Garland

On the first night of Yule, cook some popcorn. Any variety will do. Wait until it's cooled and sprinkle some sugar and salt over it as you recite these words:

> *Popcorn, banish money woe,*
> *salt cleared with a pop, pop, pop.*
> *To me fresh money will flow,*
> *money as sugar is sweet a lot, lot, lot.*
> *Money, flow now to me.*
> *An' it harm none, so mote it be.*

Then, with a needle and some gold thread, sew five pieces of popcorn together to create a long dangly garland charm. Secure it with a green ribbon and keep it safe with financial records. You could also hang one up in your office or place of work. After Yule has finished, throw the popcorn on the fire or bury it in the garden, giving thanks to all the goodness it brought during Yule.

IMBOLC
February 1–2
Meaning: Arrival of Spring
Key Term: The Quickening
Elementals: Lady of the Lake, Leprechauns
Colors: Green, White

The "festival of lights," or Imbolc, is the first stirrings of spring. The snowdrops are showing their delicate heads, and the crocus can show its head at Imbolc, too. There are so many snowdrops at this time that I have often called Imbolc "the snowdrop festival." To celebrate, you can light a white candle anointed with rosemary, bay, or basil oil. If you live in an apartment and have no garden, try to buy a little pot with a crocus or snowdrops in it. Do not go out into nature and rip them up from their place of living for a ritual. A word of warning from my own Celtic ancestors: never pick anything white and bring it into the house, as anything white in nature belongs to the goddess.

Imbolc Spell

Near a snowdrop plant, place one white candle and one yellow candle. As you light them on Imbolc, say,

> *Blessed glory to Imbolc.*
> *Awaken now to winter take.*
> *All life of spring, summer, and fall.*
> *Risen to magic, elementals all.*
> *Spreading cheer and in view.*
> *Grant this quickening of life anew.*

Keep the candles burning as long as you can until you blow them out, and watch the smoke rise through the air. Imagine it reaching the elementals of the earth as they wake from their winter slumber.

Imbolc Embrace the Flow of Money into Your Life Spell

Embrace new money coming into your life with the power of Imbolc. Place three coins in a dish in front of the snow-drops and candles, saying,

> *Gold and silver shining bright,*
> *Imbolc, grant me riches tonight.*

Keep the coins in the dish and, for seven nights, recite the spell over them.

You can always boost your chance of riches by getting a lottery ticket and placing the coins over it.

Imbolc Invocation Spell

This spell is best said outdoors. Raise your hands to the sky in a *Y* shape on February 2. Say these words to invoke the change of the season within.

> *Divine light returning to the earth,*
> *send darkness from my sight.*

I open up to changes with mirth,
love, laughter, and light.
Enter now this place.
I invoke all the Imbolc grace.

Imbolc Forget-Me-Not Spell

Buy a packet of forget-me-not seeds and sow them in a little plant pot in the house. Sow the seeds on February 2. As you sprinkle the seeds, say these words:

Lady Imbolc, fair and wise.
Hear my plea, rise to the skies.
Little seeds grow a lot.
Let him/her/them forget-me-not.

Tend the seeds and watch them grow, then give the grown plant to your beloved. Every time they look at it, they will remember you.

OSTARA
March 20–25
Meaning: Vernal Equinox
Key Term: Change of Guard
Elementals: Merfolk, Selkies
Colors: Blue, Yellow

Ostara is the modern celebration of the spring equinox when both day and night are of equal length. My family plants the seeds that have been gathered at the last harvest, and we also spring-clean the house from top to bottom. There is new life everywhere, and so the egg has become a symbol of Ostara. For your altar, you could decorate with spring flowers, such as daffodils and narcissi. The Ostara candle should be yellow; Ostara herbs, flowers, and oils include lily of the valley, jasmine, marjoram, honeysuckle, and lemon.

Ostara Blessing the Garden Spell

During Ostara, go out into the garden and perform the blessing spell to make sure you have a beautiful and bountiful garden all spring, summer, and fall. With bare feet, crouch down and place your open palm in the soil. Say,

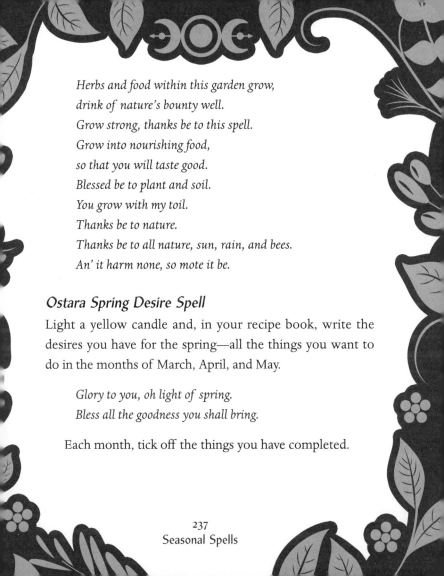

Herbs and food within this garden grow,
drink of nature's bounty well.
Grow strong, thanks be to this spell.
Grow into nourishing food,
so that you will taste good.
Blessed be to plant and soil.
You grow with my toil.
Thanks be to nature.
Thanks be to all nature, sun, rain, and bees.
An' it harm none, so mote it be.

Ostara Spring Desire Spell

Light a yellow candle and, in your recipe book, write the desires you have for the spring—all the things you want to do in the months of March, April, and May.

Glory to you, oh light of spring.
Bless all the goodness you shall bring.

Each month, tick off the things you have completed.

Oomancy Spell

Oomancy is the practice of scrying or divination with egg whites. Although it is messy, oomancy is actually quite fun. There are two ways of performing oomancy: one is to pierce an egg and hold it over a clear glass of water. As the white of the egg oozes into the water, it will make shapes. The other way is the traditional way: pierce the egg and hold it over a bowl of hot water (preferably a dark-bottomed bowl, as this enables you to see the shapes better). As the egg white drips into the boiling water, say,

> *Show what hides from me.*
> *Egg in water clarity.*

If you have a particular question, ask it at this time, and see what the egg says. If you happen to break the egg, don't worry; you can still use the whites of the egg, but never the yolk.

The egg white forms shapes in the water, which are then interpreted. Here is a list of common symbols and their meanings. Enjoy your oomancy.

Anchor: success in business, good luck, prosperity, and a secure relationship.

Birds: news from a distance. They can also mean journeys. Check your investments.

Crescent moon: romance.

Dashes: energy and a new project.

Dots: money, windfall, legacy, or salary increase.

Eye: look before you leap!

Face: a friend comes.

Gate: opportunities await you.

House: success in business or a new home.

Ivy: happiness and patience.

Jug: good health and money-making.

Key: money and other circumstances improve.

Lightning: bad weather on the horizon, so batten down the hatches, as they say.

Mermaid: misfortune for those at sea.

Nail: toothache and dentistry.

Obelisk: honor and wealth.

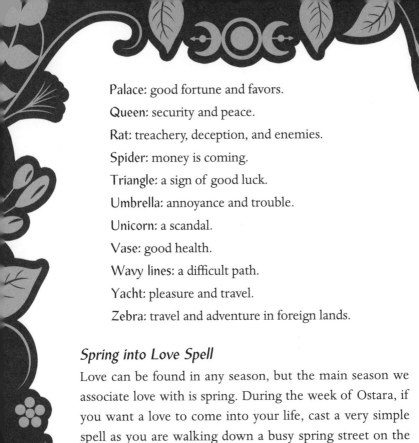

Palace: good fortune and favors.

Queen: security and peace.

Rat: treachery, deception, and enemies.

Spider: money is coming.

Triangle: a sign of good luck.

Umbrella: annoyance and trouble.

Unicorn: a scandal.

Vase: good health.

Wavy lines: a difficult path.

Yacht: pleasure and travel.

Zebra: travel and adventure in foreign lands.

Spring into Love Spell

Love can be found in any season, but the main season we associate love with is spring. During the week of Ostara, if you want a love to come into your life, cast a very simple spell as you are walking down a busy spring street on the way to work or going about your daily chores. Simply say under your breath and in your mind,

Come on, spring,
love to me you need to bring.

The first person you make eye contact with, smile, and see if they ask you out.

BELTANE
April 30–May 2
Meaning: Fertility of Earth
Key Term: The Passion
Elementals: Dragons, Salamanders
Colors: Red, Orange

Beltane falls at the time of May Day, which is a wonderful spring festival. My family often calls it "the fire festival" due to the bonfires that are lit. It is also the spring festival of merrymaking. Traditionally Beltane begins at sunset on April 30 and lasts for a couple of days until after May Day. This day, of course, has long been a celebration of fertility and dancing, notably around the Maypole, which we still use.

Beltane Passion Spell

Share a cup of wine with your intended and say this May Day incantation:

> *Blessed Beltane, threefold true and bountiful.*
> *Bless everything within my dwelling.*
> *Bless from Samhain Eve to Beltane Eve.*
> *Be the maiden, mother, and crone.*
> *Be the wild spirit of the forest.*
> *Protecting me in truth and surroundings.*
> *I ask for your blessings in this day of life.*
> *Blessed be this day of Beltane.*
> *Blessed be your light of fire.*
> *Shine upon me in the moment of desire.*

Drink the cup of wine and enjoy what the night may bring.

Beltane Ideal Partner Spell

For seven nights before you go to bed, perform this ritual. Light a white candle anointed with musk oil and say,

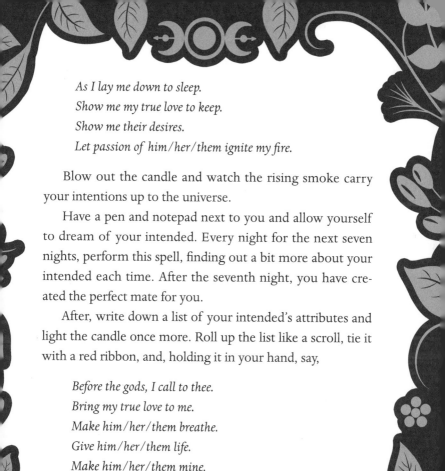

> *As I lay me down to sleep.*
> *Show me my true love to keep.*
> *Show me their desires.*
> *Let passion of him/her/them ignite my fire.*

Blow out the candle and watch the rising smoke carry your intentions up to the universe.

Have a pen and notepad next to you and allow yourself to dream of your intended. Every night for the next seven nights, perform this spell, finding out a bit more about your intended each time. After the seventh night, you have created the perfect mate for you.

After, write down a list of your intended's attributes and light the candle once more. Roll up the list like a scroll, tie it with a red ribbon, and, holding it in your hand, say,

> *Before the gods, I call to thee.*
> *Bring my true love to me.*
> *Make him/her/them breathe.*
> *Give him/her/them life.*
> *Make him/her/them mine.*
> *Mighty gods, make our two souls one.*

Beltane Forever Love Candle

This is a rather potent spell, so be sure that you want to be with the one you are with for now and evermore. Spells can turn out in ways we could never have imagined, so be careful what you cast for!

Use a peach-colored candle, and anoint it with one drop each of myrrh, jasmine, and sandalwood essential oils. As you do, say these words:

> *Candle magic, candle flame,*
> *Beltane light. Enlighten love.*
> *My beloved I shall name.*
> *Let [name] and I be of one heart.*
> *For now, and evermore.*
> *An' it harm none, so mote it be.*

Leave the candle burning for as long as possible, then extinguish it with a candlesnuffer.

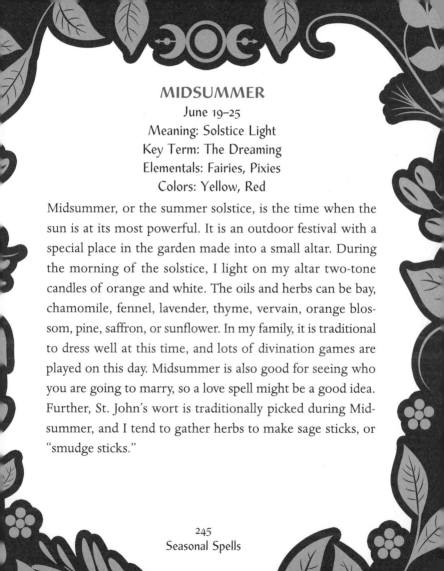

MIDSUMMER

June 19–25
Meaning: Solstice Light
Key Term: The Dreaming
Elementals: Fairies, Pixies
Colors: Yellow, Red

Midsummer, or the summer solstice, is the time when the sun is at its most powerful. It is an outdoor festival with a special place in the garden made into a small altar. During the morning of the solstice, I light on my altar two-tone candles of orange and white. The oils and herbs can be bay, chamomile, fennel, lavender, thyme, vervain, orange blossom, pine, saffron, or sunflower. In my family, it is traditional to dress well at this time, and lots of divination games are played on this day. Midsummer is also good for seeing who you are going to marry, so a love spell might be a good idea. Further, St. John's wort is traditionally picked during Midsummer, and I tend to gather herbs to make sage sticks, or "smudge sticks."

Midsummer Spell

Take a piece of jewelry that you like the most. Lighting one red and one yellow candle, place your piece of jewelry between the two candles and say these words:

> Midsummer spirits, I call upon thee.
> Enchant this jewelry to all those who see.
> Make it twinkle with fairy might.
> Falling in love with me on sight.
> Grant this wish for me.
> An' it harm none, so mote it be.

Wear the piece of jewelry all throughout the celebration of Midsummer. Afterward, give thanks to the fairies for the magic it brought and sprinkle some of your magic salt over it to cleanse it.

Midsummer's Eve Love Spell

Use hawthorn blossom to foresee the future and, in particular, your future lover. Sprinkle some hawthorn flowers over a mirror that you only use for magic. Then light one yellow candle and one black candle. Say these words into your mirror:

Blossom night, blossom white.
Gracious lady, thank you for your gifts this night.
I wish I may, I wish I might.
Grant me the gift of foresight.
The future I would see, a love just for me.
An' it harm none, so mote it be.

Lamb's Ear Fairy Sight Spell

If you are fortunate enough to grow lamb's ear in your garden, cast a spell of innocence over it. In your night garden, light a golden candle and, sitting on the ground, say these words:

In this hour and on this night.
Let me see childlike.
The wonder and magic of fairy sight.

Touch the leaves of the lamb's ear and close your eyes. Gently touch each eyelid with your index finger. Then open them, and allow yourself to see the wonder of the night.

Midsummer Lucky Day Charm

All families need a little luck sometimes, and any day that ends in a *Y* is a lucky day. Family charms are ideal to make as a family, especially as the youngest members of the family can color them.

Draw a four-leaf clover on a piece of green cardstock and cut it out. Sprinkle some Midsummer blossoms or flowers over it. Light a green candle and say these words:

> *Green is the color that makes it right,*
> *green is the color of good luck both day and night.*
> *Little charm of Midsummer,*
> *bring to this home luck forever.*

Focus on the candle and your charm, and imagine the Midsummer light streaming into the charm, bringing good luck. Give thanks to the universe and blow out the candle. Keep your good luck charm in your purse or wallet. Another way to keep the good luck in the family is to hang the charm in the house, especially in the kitchen, as the kitchen represents the heart of the home and family.

LAMMAS

July 31–August 2
Meaning: Harvest
Key Term: The Wake
Elementals: Unicorns, Pegasus
Colors: Black, Brown

For some reason, Lammas always seems a bit of a depressing festival to me. It is the first festival of the harvest, a clear indication that autumn is on its way. Lammas is usually represented by wheat, so loaves of bread, corn dollies, and sunflowers, which are also out in abundance in August, all represent this festival.

Lammas Loaf Blessing for Health, Wealth, and Prosperity

Over a fresh loaf surrounded by early fruits, such as raspberries and plums, hold out open palms and say,

> *Harvest blessing of first fruits.*
> *Nature's gifts you bring.*
> *Health and wealth and prosperity, too,*
> *Lammas gods, I ask of you.*

Lammas Travel Spell

Travel with a piece of turquoise jewelry on you or carry a piece of turquoise in a bag or purse. This is the stone of protection when traveling. Holding a piece of turquoise in your hands, recite this spell:

> *Traveling here, traveling there,*
> *traveling absolutely everywhere.*
> *Blessed Mercury, keep me safe,*
> *in all my travels, wherever I am bound.*
> *By sea, in the air, or on the ground.*
> *An' it harm none, so mote it be.*

Carry the turquoise with you whenever you are traveling.

Lammas Mock Orange Positivity Spell

Write your suffering friend's name in blue ink on a piece of paper. Alternatively, if you are suffering, write your own name.

Lighting a blue candle, inhale the scent of the mock orange, roll up the paper, and hold it in your hands. Recite these words:

Into the light you / I must come.
Drive the darkness from your / my sight.
No more fear and no more dread.
Negative thoughts banish from your / my head.

Keep hold of the paper, then bury it in the soil of the mock orange plant.

MABON
September 20–25
Meaning: Equinox
Key Term: The Bounty
Elementals: Sphinx, Sylphs
Colors: Brown, Orange

Mabon, or "harvest home," is the modern celebration of the autumnal equinox. In my family, it is the first festival of autumn and the start of winter preparations. It is viewed as a time of contemplation. We also call it "the apple festival," as we traditionally pick the orchard fruits now. Mabon is regarded as one of the most powerful magical periods of the year.

Mabon Spell

This festival is the marker of past, present, and future, so spells of time are perfect at Mabon—either blessings and gratitude for the past year, or the creation of a spell for the future. Light one black and one white candle and say these words:

> *Changing seasons, seasons past,*
> *let the future hold what's true at last.*
> *Let all my dreams come true.*
> *Let all my adventures be new.*
> *Blessed Mabon, let it be.*
> *An' it harm none, so mote it be.*

Think of five things that have happened to you in the year since last Samhain, then list five goals you have for the coming year. Write them all down on a piece of yellow paper. Keep the paper in a safe place, and next Mabon, you can take it out and see what you have accomplished. Give thanks and burn the paper as you repeat the Mabon future spell above.

Mabon Sylph Spell

Holding your schoolbooks, invoke a sylph to help and guide you through this academic year.

> *Being of knowledge, being of air.*
> *Grant me success this year.*
> *At school I must toil throughout.*
> *My goals, there is no doubt.*
> *Mabon sylph, I ask this of thee.*
> *An' it harm none, so mote it be.*

When you feel yourself struggling to understand things at school, call upon your teachers first for clarity, and then ask your sylph to help you make sense of the task.

Mabon Apple Slice Spell

Slice one green apple in half through its middle, not downward from the stem. This will reveal a pentagram in each slice. Continue to slice that way a couple of times. Try to cut five slices. Leave the apple slices for a couple of days to completely dry out. They should look and feel a bit like leather.

Next, draw the pentagram on a piece of green paper (or on white paper with a green pen). Light a green candle. Place four apple slices on the pentagram, leaving the top point empty, as that represents spirit, or the divine. Say these words:

Green apple, offerings of pentagram might,
help my purse be not so light.
Dear goddess of Mabon,
bestow your gifts of financial plenty.
Mabon apple, bring prosperity.
An' it harm none, so mote it be.

Keep the candle burning as long as possible. Focus your thoughts on money coming into your life like the rays of light coming from the candle. Keep one of the apple slices in your purse. You could give the others to friends who may have need of them.

ESBATS

An esbat is the ritual acknowledging the full moon. However, it is also worth bearing in mind that the full moon is not just one night, it is a set of three nights—the night before, during, and after the actual full moon. It is entirely up to the individual what exactly they wish to perform during a full moon, be it a healing ritual, divination, or spell weaving.

I assign a different purpose to each of the three nights of a full moon. The first night is a gratitude ritual in which I list the things I am grateful for for that month. The second night is usually a healing spell for someone or for the earth if there have been natural disasters, such as fires and floods. The third night is a spell just for me, which focuses on money, career, or love. You can choose how you want to celebrate the full moon days; remember, no two hedgewitches are the same. There are many choices, and it is entirely up to you. Here is one idea to get you started.

The Moon Pot Esbat Spell

Create a moon garden pot with plants that specifically come out at night, and use it to open an esbat ceremony.

> *North, south, east, and west.*
> *Here in my garden is best.*
> *By day or by night.*

The great work of magic is right.
So, blessings all to one and thee.
An' it harm none, so mote it be.

During the recital of the spell, when you say "thee," raise your hands up to the full moon.

The Last Word

The stereotypical image of the witch in her kitchen, surrounded by bottles and herbs, potions, and spells, brewing up magic, gave rise to herbal benefits and discoveries. The time-old benefits of chewing willow bark for pains or fevers is now realized, and aspirin is the derivative of this practice. I owe so much to the shamans and medicine men and women of the past with their knowledge of herbs, the world, and their belief system.

However, magic is the beginning of science, for without magic, questions would never be asked, and reason and research would never come to light. As human beings progress further and further with their technological discoveries,

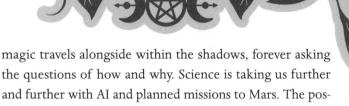

magic travels alongside within the shadows, forever asking the questions of how and why. Science is taking us further and further with AI and planned missions to Mars. The possibilities are endless.

Magic is promiscuous; it will go with anything. It is our past, our present, and our future. When we finally leave this planet and venture far into the universe on our spaceships and rockets, magic will go with us. We will see the wonder of new worlds and begin asking those same questions all over again.

In this book, we have looked at the areas most prevalent in our lives and our world. We have discovered correspondences to be used in all these subjects. Use them and try to write your own spells, thinking of the correspondences as pieces of thread that you are going to use to weave your own magic. Your spells are your own creation. Some can rhyme, but they do not have to. You can honor the gods or just the universe. Remember always to write down all your spells and magical work in your recipe book.

The easiest thing to understand about a spell is that it's "a command to the universe," whatever you deem that to be, for something to happen. Spell making is a form of spell weaving, as the universe has many intricate components within it, which we use to spin magic. Spells are collections of words or commands. We start by describing the problem and how we want it to be resolved magically, and, generally, we close the spell by saying, "So mote it be." Many spells have a rhyming tone to them, because this adds a rhythm to them, which holds power. The more you say and repeat it, the stronger the spell—you are enforcing your will onto something. That is why it is so important that you act with responsibility.

If I wanted to write a spell about money, I would break it down into steps. The first step is identifying the problem: I have no money at the end of the month. What is the desired outcome? I want some money at the end of the month. This becomes,

At the end of the month, money I have none.
At the end of this month, I would like some.

You can, of course, change "month" to "week" if needs be, but you are not putting a figure on how much money

you want, because you are allowing the universe to give you what you really need to get by until the end of the month or until you get paid again. You want to make your command specific; however, you also want to show that you're honest and acting with responsibly. Thus,

> *At the end of the month, money I have none.*
> *At the end of this week, I would like some,*
> *so that I may pay bills and have what I need.*
> *To the universe, I show no greed.*

Now, you need to show that the spell is finished, and that it will harm no one. Spells have a way of turning out in a certain manner, so we always put in a clause that no one will be harmed or hurt by our command. Our completed spell would look something like this:

> *At the end of the month, money I have none.*
> *At the end of this week, I would like some,*
> *so that I may pay bills and have what I need.*
> *To the universe, I show no greed.*
> *An' it harm none, so mote it be.*

We have made a spell, and we could just repeat it—but let us do some weaving, using threads within the universe. Remember that giant spiderweb? Think of the correspondences and everything in this world and the unseen world as a strand on that giant spiderweb. Green is the color of money, so light a green candle while reciting the spell. The day is important, too, and Friday is a good day to begin this work. We need to recite this spell every night for a week—from Friday to Friday—while lighting the green candle. Now, try writing a spell of your own, and always make sure to write your spells in your recipe book.

First and foremost, though, remember always that you are in control of your magic. Use the Craft wisely and responsibly—and be careful what you cast for.

A Witch's Dictionary

There are so many words and phrases that are used in hedge-witchery that you may or may not know. Therefore, I have devised this dictionary of some of the more obscure terms used in traditional spell work. Many have been forgotten by time.

A word of warning: I have included the names of some herbs here that can be used for medicinal or magical purposes, but you should always check their properties and consult a physician before using them. If in doubt, *do not* use them. Always act responsibly!

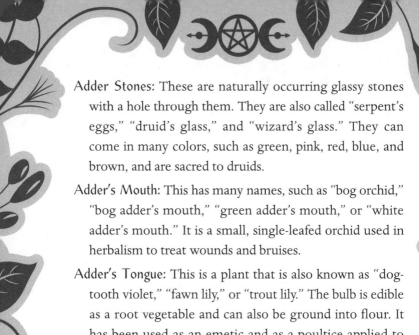

Adder Stones: These are naturally occurring glassy stones with a hole through them. They are also called "serpent's eggs," "druid's glass," and "wizard's glass." They can come in many colors, such as green, pink, red, blue, and brown, and are sacred to druids.

Adder's Mouth: This has many names, such as "bog orchid," "bog adder's mouth," "green adder's mouth," or "white adder's mouth." It is a small, single-leafed orchid used in herbalism to treat wounds and bruises.

Adder's Tongue: This is a plant that is also known as "dog-tooth violet," "fawn lily," or "trout lily." The bulb is edible as a root vegetable and can also be ground into flour. It has been used as an emetic and as a poultice applied to tumors and ulcers.

Angelica: A large flowering plant with a pleasant perfume, valued for its flavor in liquors and as a remedy for colds and rheumatism. More importantly, as the name implies, it attracts angels and banishes demons.

Amulet: There are so many amulets, and every culture, time, and people have at least one that is significant to them.

An amulet is an object that is given great power either to ward off evil or to protect the wearer or the house.

Besom: Another name for a broomstick. A stick that consists of twigs around one end, used to sweep leaves and dirt.

Blocula: A site in Sweden that was a large meadow where the Mora witches went to perform their rituals. This case of witch hysteria and the subsequent trials are an excellent example of mass hysteria to study, as over three hundred children were involved; the hysteria also managed to engulf Finland.

Brocken: One of the most famous places in Germany for the sabbat of Walpurgis Night on April 30.

Buying Wind: What a lovely term for storm raising, and, yes, witches are alleged to be responsible for making storms. Buying wind, of course, is witches making deals with the devil to raise a storm that will destroy harvests, crops, houses, or even kings at sea!

Captoptromancy: This is another term for scrying. Using mirrors, flames, fires, or water to see events, either future or past (not to mention present).

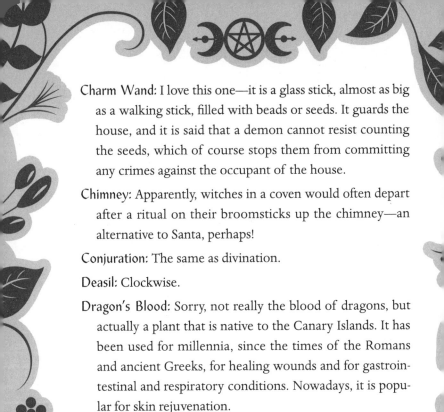

Charm Wand: I love this one—it is a glass stick, almost as big as a walking stick, filled with beads or seeds. It guards the house, and it is said that a demon cannot resist counting the seeds, which of course stops them from committing any crimes against the occupant of the house.

Chimney: Apparently, witches in a coven would often depart after a ritual on their broomsticks up the chimney—an alternative to Santa, perhaps!

Conjuration: The same as divination.

Deasil: Clockwise.

Dragon's Blood: Sorry, not really the blood of dragons, but actually a plant that is native to the Canary Islands. It has been used for millennia, since the times of the Romans and ancient Greeks, for healing wounds and for gastrointestinal and respiratory conditions. Nowadays, it is popular for skin rejuvenation.

Elf Shot: An unexpected decline in the health of someone in the local village, said of course to be the work of witches or fairies under the guidance of a witch. In other words, it is a witch's curse.

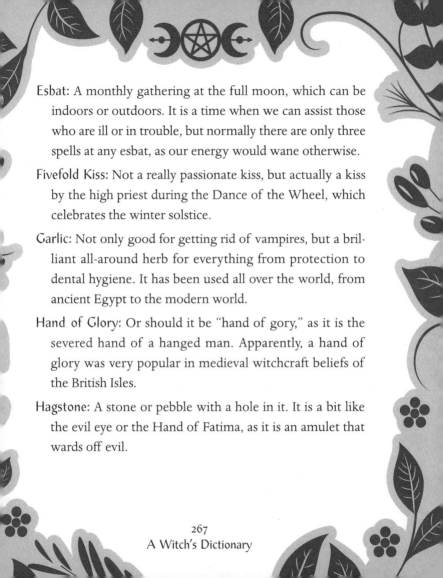

Esbat: A monthly gathering at the full moon, which can be indoors or outdoors. It is a time when we can assist those who are ill or in trouble, but normally there are only three spells at any esbat, as our energy would wane otherwise.

Fivefold Kiss: Not a really passionate kiss, but actually a kiss by the high priest during the Dance of the Wheel, which celebrates the winter solstice.

Garlic: Not only good for getting rid of vampires, but a brilliant all-around herb for everything from protection to dental hygiene. It has been used all over the world, from ancient Egypt to the modern world.

Hand of Glory: Or should it be "hand of gory," as it is the severed hand of a hanged man. Apparently, a hand of glory was very popular in medieval witchcraft beliefs of the British Isles.

Hagstone: A stone or pebble with a hole in it. It is a bit like the evil eye or the Hand of Fatima, as it is an amulet that wards off evil.

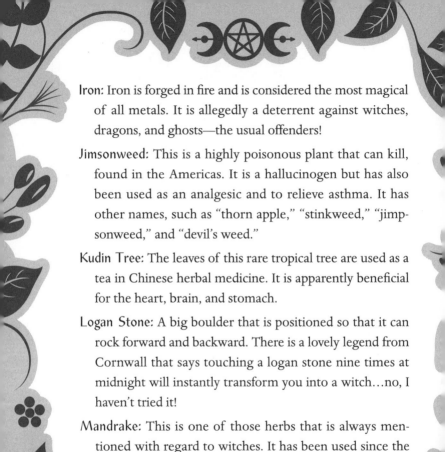

Iron: Iron is forged in fire and is considered the most magical of all metals. It is allegedly a deterrent against witches, dragons, and ghosts—the usual offenders!

Jimsonweed: This is a highly poisonous plant that can kill, found in the Americas. It is a hallucinogen but has also been used as an analgesic and to relieve asthma. It has other names, such as "thorn apple," "stinkweed," "jimp-sonweed," and "devil's weed."

Kudin Tree: The leaves of this rare tropical tree are used as a tea in Chinese herbal medicine. It is apparently beneficial for the heart, brain, and stomach.

Logan Stone: A big boulder that is positioned so that it can rock forward and backward. There is a lovely legend from Cornwall that says touching a logan stone nine times at midnight will instantly transform you into a witch...no, I haven't tried it!

Mandrake: This is one of those herbs that is always mentioned with regard to witches. It has been used since the beginning of time as an aphrodisiac and a major contribution in sex magic. So much so that in England, we called

it "love apples," though in past centuries the fruit was also called "the devil's apples." But take care—this is a highly poisonous plant and is extremely toxic and dangerous.

Mirrors: There are many superstitions. Many of the ancients believed that when a person looked into a mirror, their soul would move into the reflection. In Victorian times, a broken mirror was said to mean the death of a family member or friend. Mirrors are often used in scrying and meditation.

Nightshade: We call it "deadly nightshade," and it is precisely that. The berries of this herbaceous shrub contain belladonna, which is a hallucinogen and can also be highly toxic. In certain preparations, however, it has many medicinal uses, such as pain relief and reducing inflammation. Belladonna was one of the key components in the witch's "flying" potion of yesteryear.

Oak: This tree is sacred to all, but we have many superstitions regarding it, such as hammering a nail into the poor tree to relieve you of a toothache. People also believed that the oak tree could ward off evil spirits, so much so that some people would wear oak leaves, while others

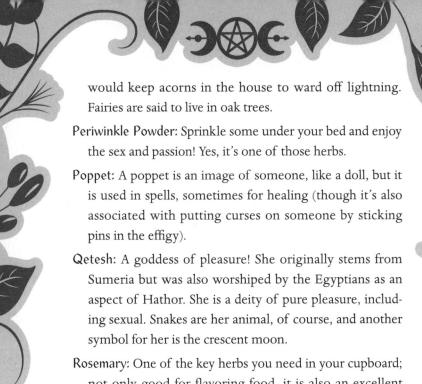

would keep acorns in the house to ward off lightning. Fairies are said to live in oak trees.

Periwinkle Powder: Sprinkle some under your bed and enjoy the sex and passion! Yes, it's one of those herbs.

Poppet: A poppet is an image of someone, like a doll, but it is used in spells, sometimes for healing (though it's also associated with putting curses on someone by sticking pins in the effigy).

Qetesh: A goddess of pleasure! She originally stems from Sumeria but was also worshiped by the Egyptians as an aspect of Hathor. She is a deity of pure pleasure, including sexual. Snakes are her animal, of course, and another symbol for her is the crescent moon.

Rosemary: One of the key herbs you need in your cupboard; not only good for flavoring food, it is also an excellent herb for love enchantments and can be used in spells provoking lust.

Samson Root: A purple coneflower. The root was used to treat stings and snakebites. It is a component of echinacea and said to strengthen the immune system. It also increases virility, allegedly, so carry some in your pocket.

Silver: Regarded as one of the most pure and potent of all metals. Apart from the killing of werewolves, it is also good for getting rid of witches, as normal bullets can be warded off by spells, but silver cannot be corrupted by magic.

Sow Thistle: Also known as "hare thistle." This is a common weed surprisingly rich in vitamins and minerals, used in herbal medicine to treat liver and kidney ailments, among others. It can also be helpful in invisibility spells. No, haven't tried that either!

Stonecrop: This one is quite self-explanatory: it is a flower that grows on the side of rocks or walls. In the past, it has been used to treat epilepsy and skin diseases. But please remember to always consult a physician before treating any ailment with herbs.

Toadflax: A weed, also known as "devil's ribbon," used in herbal medicine as an astringent and diuretic. A very good plant for breaking hexes, too.

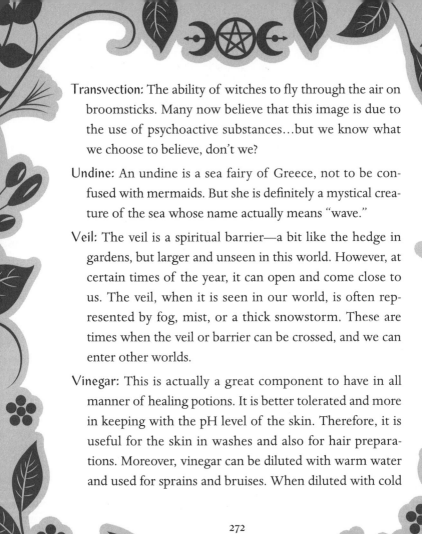

Transvection: The ability of witches to fly through the air on broomsticks. Many now believe that this image is due to the use of psychoactive substances…but we know what we choose to believe, don't we?

Undine: An undine is a sea fairy of Greece, not to be confused with mermaids. But she is definitely a mystical creature of the sea whose name actually means "wave."

Veil: The veil is a spiritual barrier—a bit like the hedge in gardens, but larger and unseen in this world. However, at certain times of the year, it can open and come close to us. The veil, when it is seen in our world, is often represented by fog, mist, or a thick snowstorm. These are times when the veil or barrier can be crossed, and we can enter other worlds.

Vinegar: This is actually a great component to have in all manner of healing potions. It is better tolerated and more in keeping with the pH level of the skin. Therefore, it is useful for the skin in washes and also for hair preparations. Moreover, vinegar can be diluted with warm water and used for sprains and bruises. When diluted with cold

or iced water, it becomes an excellent compress for tension headaches or hot swollen joints.

Widdershins: This means anticlockwise, or steering something in the opposite direction, while deasil literally means "right" and is the direction one turns when going clockwise.

Willow: These trees are said to uproot themselves and follow you through the woods at night. You have been warned.

X: On the Gardnerian pentacle, there are three X-shaped crosses that represent those anointing in an initiation ceremony.

Youth: The Celtic deity of youth was also the deity of healing, water, beauty, writing, and magic, among other things. He was known by many titles, such as "Cloud Maker," "Silver Hand," and, my favorite, "He Who Bestows Wealth." His name is Nuada.

Zodiac: I could have started this witch's dictionary with astrology, but, instead, I now end it with zodiac. Every country has a zodiac of some kind. Here in the West, we have twelve signs of the zodiac: three water signs, three earth signs, three air signs, and three fire signs—the elements are everywhere! However, there is also Chinese astrology with their animal signs, while in India, they have Vedic astrology. Research them all and have fun looking into them. Remember, learn everything you can. Knowledge is free, so listen and learn.

Bibliography

Binney, Ruth. *Wise Words & Country Ways: For House & Home*. Exeter, UK: David & Charles Newton Abbott, 2000.

——. *Wise Words & Country Ways: Weather Lore*. Exeter, UK: David & Charles Newton Abbott, 2010.

Castleden, Rodney. *The Element Encyclopaedia of the Celts: The Ultimate A-Z of the Symbols, History, and Spirituality of the Legendary Celts*. Glasgow: Harper Collins, 2012.

Conway, D. J. *Celtic Magic*. Woodbury, MN: Llewellyn Publications, 1990.

——. *Norse Magic*. Woodbury, MN: Llewellyn Publications, 1990.

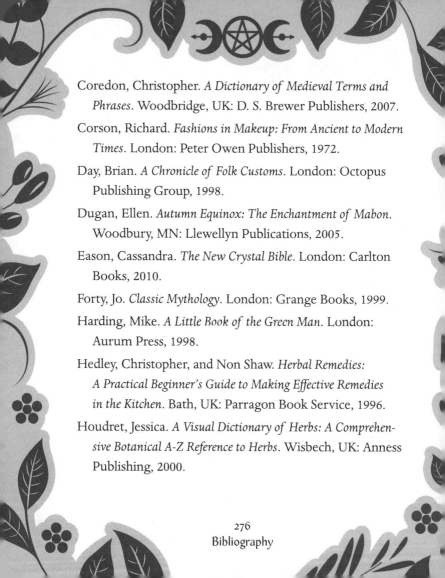

Coredon, Christopher. *A Dictionary of Medieval Terms and Phrases*. Woodbridge, UK: D. S. Brewer Publishers, 2007.

Corson, Richard. *Fashions in Makeup: From Ancient to Modern Times*. London: Peter Owen Publishers, 1972.

Day, Brian. *A Chronicle of Folk Customs*. London: Octopus Publishing Group, 1998.

Dugan, Ellen. *Autumn Equinox: The Enchantment of Mabon*. Woodbury, MN: Llewellyn Publications, 2005.

Eason, Cassandra. *The New Crystal Bible*. London: Carlton Books, 2010.

Forty, Jo. *Classic Mythology*. London: Grange Books, 1999.

Harding, Mike. *A Little Book of the Green Man*. London: Aurum Press, 1998.

Hedley, Christopher, and Non Shaw. *Herbal Remedies: A Practical Beginner's Guide to Making Effective Remedies in the Kitchen*. Bath, UK: Parragon Book Service, 1996.

Houdret, Jessica. *A Visual Dictionary of Herbs: A Comprehensive Botanical A-Z Reference to Herbs*. Wisbech, UK: Anness Publishing, 2000.

Kershaw, Stephen P. *The Greek Myths: Gods, Monsters, Heroes and the Origins of Storytelling*. London: Constable & Robinson, 2007.

Leland, C. G. *Aradia: Gospel of the Witches*. London: David Butt, 1899.

March, Jenny. *The Penguin Book of Classical Myths*. London: Penguin Books, 2008.

Mathews, John. *The Quest for the Green Man*. Wheaton, IL: Quest Books, 2001.

Meadows, Kenneth. *The Little Library of Earth Medicine*. London: DK Publishing, 1998.

Michael, Pamela. *Edible Wild Plants and Herbs*. London: Ernest Benn, 1980.

Moorey, Teresa. *The Fairy Bible*. London: Octopus Publishing Group, 2008.

Nozedar, Adele. *The Element Encyclopaedia of Secret Signs and Symbols: The Ultimate A-Z Guide from Alchemy to Zodiac*. London: Harper Element, 2008.

O'Rush, Claire. *The Enchanted Garden*. London: Random House, 2000.

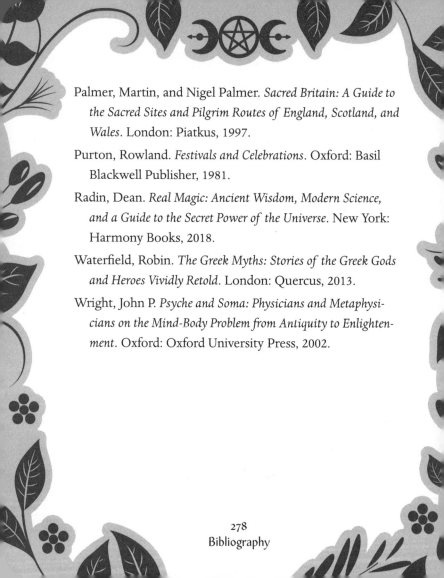

Palmer, Martin, and Nigel Palmer. *Sacred Britain: A Guide to the Sacred Sites and Pilgrim Routes of England, Scotland, and Wales*. London: Piatkus, 1997.

Purton, Rowland. *Festivals and Celebrations*. Oxford: Basil Blackwell Publisher, 1981.

Radin, Dean. *Real Magic: Ancient Wisdom, Modern Science, and a Guide to the Secret Power of the Universe*. New York: Harmony Books, 2018.

Waterfield, Robin. *The Greek Myths: Stories of the Greek Gods and Heroes Vividly Retold*. London: Quercus, 2013.

Wright, John P. *Psyche and Soma: Physicians and Metaphysicians on the Mind-Body Problem from Antiquity to Enlightenment*. Oxford: Oxford University Press, 2002.

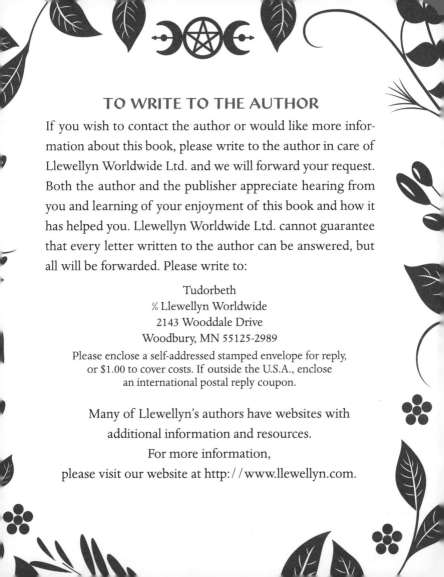

TO WRITE TO THE AUTHOR

If you wish to contact the author or would like more information about this book, please write to the author in care of Llewellyn Worldwide Ltd. and we will forward your request. Both the author and the publisher appreciate hearing from you and learning of your enjoyment of this book and how it has helped you. Llewellyn Worldwide Ltd. cannot guarantee that every letter written to the author can be answered, but all will be forwarded. Please write to:

Tudorbeth
℅ Llewellyn Worldwide
2143 Wooddale Drive
Woodbury, MN 55125-2989

Please enclose a self-addressed stamped envelope for reply,
or $1.00 to cover costs. If outside the U.S.A., enclose
an international postal reply coupon.

Many of Llewellyn's authors have websites with
additional information and resources.
For more information,
please visit our website at http://www.llewellyn.com.

NOTES

_____

_____

_____

_____

_____

_____

_____

_____

_____

_____

NOTES

_____

_____

_____

_____

_____

_____

_____

_____

_____

_____

NOTES

_____

_____

_____

_____

_____

_____

_____

_____

_____

_____

_____

NOTES

_____

_____

_____

_____

_____

_____

_____

_____

_____

_____

NOTES

_____

_____

_____

_____

_____

_____

_____

_____

_____

_____

NOTES

_____

_____

_____

_____

_____

_____

_____

_____

_____

_____

_____

NOTES

_____

_____

_____

_____

_____

_____

_____

_____

_____

_____

_____